Why They Stay and Why They Go

Attracting and Retaining Employees

WILLIAM A. HOWATT

Howatt HR Consulting Inc.

ISBN 978-1-894338-19-6

Published 2008

Howatt HR Consulting Inc.
6585 Hwy. 221
Kentville NS B4N 3V7

Preface

A landmark study by Dr. Nick Bontis (2001), done in partnership with Accenture, Institute for Intellectual Capital Research, and Saratoga Institute, reported the following: 1) The development of senior management leadership capabilities is the key starting ingredient for the reduction in turnover rates and the retention of key employees; 2) Business performance is positively influenced by the commitment of its members, and their ability to generate new knowledge directly reduces turnover that has a positive impact on the workforce.

Research like this and other studies on human capital continue to show that if, on average, businesses spend 40% of their revenue on employee salaries and benefits it's important to understand what motivates and influences a workforce to want to stay or go. Leaders are realizing that no other asset will provide a stronger lever for success than having a talented and stable workforce.

Several variables are changing. The workforce is shrinking; global competition is increasing; and knowledge management and transfer are becoming much more important. It's critical also for an organization's long-term success to slow down attrition so that more resources can be used to benefit the intact workforce through effective communication, knowledge transfer, performance management, and career development — all critical for organizational success planning. Organizations now realize that due to the aging workforce and eligible retirement a large percentage of their tacit knowledge may be walking out the door in the near future. It is, therefore, becoming more important to attract and retain the right talent.

The purpose of this book is to help corporate leaders facilitate discussions at all levels of their organizations to explore and examine the reason people would want to come to work for them and why some they wish would stay are leaving. The goal is to provide leaders with strategies to influence both attraction and retention. No strategy will work unless senior management is supportive and committed to attraction and retention, two pillars that must be in place for an organization to become an employer of choice.

At the end of the day, attraction and retention take time and commitment; there are no shortcuts. But there are clear to-dos and do-nots. Each chapter in this book has been developed to provide insight on strategies and decisions that will assist a workplace in becoming a place where employees want to come and stay. By the end of this book you will be able to develop an approach to increase attraction and retention in your organization. Once this approach is completed, the next step will be implementation, commitment, measurement, and follow-through.

Contents

CHAPTER 1

Talent: A Limited Resource

Starting in 2008, we will be facing the worst labor storage in our lifetime within the next five years—Jeff Tailor, Monster

There are really two critical challenges for corporations today in regard to talent management: 1) finding enough talent, 2) keeping enough talent. Of course, keeping talent that is not effective is not much better than having no talent. The purpose of this book is to introduce leaders from all levels of organizations to insights, research, and strategies as to how to attract and retain talent. To do this it's important for leaders to have a clear understanding of the core drivers that influence why employees want to come to a company and why they leave. To be strategic as a leader it's important to have the facts and to decide on the right course of action. The cost of doing nothing today in regard to attraction and retention is simply too high. A company's long-term success is determined by its ability to attract and maintain a quality workforce.

When looking at this concept it's important for employers to be clear on the following two questions: 1) What kind worker is the right fit for this organization?; 2) What is the current profile of the workforce and what do we expect for the future? Branham (2001) explains that employees tend to fall into four categories: a) *star performers*—who are your most valuable resource and represent on average the top 10%; b) *high performers*—this group does not get as much attention as the stars but is as important and often the easiest to be recruited away as organizations often don't recognize the fact this group, which makes up 20%-30% of the organization, not only meets expectations but exceeds them; c) *steady performers*—the majority of the workforce. About 40%-50% of this group are the solid citizens; they may not be the leaders or stars but they are great followers, competent, reliable, and loyal; d) *poor/marginal performers*—these are the functionally ineffective ones who often are in the wrong role for their skill set, or they have a bad attitude and poor work ethic. In most organizations this represents as much as 15%-20% of the workforce, which is both problematic and expensive.

What is the single biggest challenge for organizations today in regard to attracting the right talent?

The answer is finding the right talent. Did you know that because of the changing demographic one-half of the more than 76 million baby boomers in North America are eligible to retire in the next 10 years and to complicate this the number of workers between the ages of 25 and 54 is shrinking (Kaye & Jordon-Evans, 2005). The authors go on to report that 56 million jobs will open up by 2012 that will require millions of hours interviewing, training, and on-boarding and millions of dollars in replacement costs. More than 75% of all corporate leaders now agree that employee retention is a major issue; however, only 15% have a plan to address it (Fishman, 1998). The author continues to point out that research has found that more than half of organizations in North America report they are noticing an increasing trend and concern regarding turnover, with only 9% reporting that their retention efforts have been successful.

Why They Leave

Engagement is a core driver that facilitates retention of talent when examining employee retention and turnover. For example, on average, 13% of the United States workforce quits to take another job each month (Clark, 1999), and for those who don't quit approximately 55% are thinking about quitting within the year (Reichheild, 1999).

All the ups and downs of the economy that have led to downsizing, reorganization, and constant change over the last 20 years have increased anxiety in the average employee about job security and resulted in many taking the position that they must look out for themselves. The result is that it has become much more complex to engage, gain long-term commitment, and motivate a workforce. Harris and Branncik (1999) report that the average professional holds more than eight jobs from the ages of 18 to 32. This is evidence of the career turmoil many employers are facing. The authors go on to suggest that a large percentage of the workforce is disconnected on three levels: company, job, and personal, and for a company's long-term success it must start to address this issue and help employees feel engaged and connected to their work. Many employees don't look at a job as a career but as a stepping stone to another opportunity that may be better for them. Gone are the days of one job equals one career until retirement.

Research based on over 20,000 workers from 18 industries and from dozens of other studies shows 80%-90% stated their number one reason for leaving was not because of money. But since approximately 90% of managers feel this is the main reason, this is clear evidence of the disconnect between what employees want and what employers think they want (Branham, 2005). The author goes on to offer his own research that provides senior executives with empirical facts that if dealt with will improve their organizations' ability to be profitable through a stable workforce:

- The job or workplace was not as expected.

- Mismatch between job and person.

- Too little coaching and feedback.

- Too few growth and advancement opportunities.

- Feel devalued and unrecognized.

- Stress from overwork and work-life imbalance.

- Loss of trust and confidence in senior leaders.

Do you know what your poach rate is?

Knowing its poach rate helps an organization find out how much it is costing to lose talent to its competitors. If your poach rate is less than 20% it is not the money that's motivating people to leave, because people who love their work, company, and boss don't leave for an offer unless it's transformational, and this amount is not (Putzier, 2001).

A Towers-Perrin study reported 85% of employees cited career advancement was a key reward but only 49% said their company was providing it; 80% stated learning and development were critical and only 50% provided it. This points out that fewer than half of companies are doing anything constructively to assist employees in career planning and professional learning. Kaye and Jordon-Evans' (2005) original research, called What Kept You, was based on more than 15,000 respondents who stated the top 10 reasons why employees stay in the workplace are:

- Exciting work challenge.

- Career growth, learning, and development.

- Working with great people.

- Fair pay.

- Supportive management and boss.

- Being recognized, valued, and respected.

- Benefits.

- Meaningful work and making a difference.

- Pride in the organization, its mission, and its product.

- Great work environment and culture.

More than 50% of an employee's job satisfaction can be directly related to the health of the relationship with their direct supervisor (Saratoga Institute, 1995). A survey reported that two-thirds of 1,290 managers interviewed did not know how to quantify the costs of turnover (Kepner-Trego, 1999). Figure 1 shows a tool managers can use for estimating turnover costs. Failure to make this kind of calculation is perhaps one reason why many don't connect the dots as to how important their behaviors are in regard to influencing turnover and how much it costs to turn over a workforce.

When a workforce perceives management as being uncaring it has a negative impact on productivity. In a recent study of 3,000 workers, 56% reported their organization failed to show concern, 45% failed to treat them fairly, 41% failed to gain their trust, and only 24% reported they were loyal (Stafford, 1998). In some cases, employees perceive their management as being abusive as well as uncaring. Smye and Wright (1996) described this as a "Culture of Sacrifice," characterized as:

- Excessive demand for personal sacrifice.

- Demand on employees to be available at home.

- Continual crisis.

- Employees subject to unreasonable deadlines.

- Pony Express management philosophy.

The result of this pressure:

- Employee burnout.

- Depression in workforce.

- Turnover.

- Absenteeism.

- Accidents.

- Costly mistakes.

- Lack of energy in workforce.

- Poor life balance.

- Retention of passive and dependent workforce.

Estimating Turnover Costs	
Direct Costs	**Actual or Estimated Costs**
Recruitment advertising	$
Internal referral bonus	$
Agency search fees	$
Applicants' expenses	$
Relocation expenses	$
Selection testing	$
Medical exam	$
Drug screening	$
Background check	$
Recruiting expenses	$
Total Direct Costs	$
Indirect Costs	
Employment office overhead	$
Staff salary and benefits for processing time	$
Management time	$
Direct supervisors' time	$
Orientation time	$
Training and resource time	$
Lost opportunity costs (estimated)	$
Learning curve productivity loss (estimated)	$
Customer service disruption and defections/lost business (estimated)	$
Total Indirect Costs	$

Examining the Value of Talent

Tangible assets such as equipment and furniture depreciate annually, with the negative effect on a company's bottom line listed as a standard projection in P&L statements. A corporation's talent assets (e.g., intellectual property and innovative ideas) have the potential to appreciate as employees gain knowledge and experience, but remain absent from financial projections in spite of the measurable impact on profits. According to research by McKinsey & Company (2001):

- Top performing portfolio managers in financial services institutions grew revenues by nearly 50% while average performers' portfolios remained flat.

- The companies that excel in talent management achieved total returns to shareholders that were 22 percentage points better than the average in their industry—*not* 22%, 22 *percentage points* better.

The concrete expenses related to turnover represent about 9% of revenue. However, a greater risk to a corporation is loss of highly competent knowledge workers. A company's best performers usually have been at the firm for 3 to 10 years and are between the ages of 25 and 35. The combined firm-specific experience of these skilled professionals forms a core of talent equity that secures repeat business from clients.

Talent value includes implicit knowledge, tacit knowledge, and skills. Research indicates that only 20% of a company's practices and procedures are written down; 8% of all the knowledge in an organization is in the heads of its workforce. If talent begins to leave faster than a company can replace and develop new people, systems begin to break down because current staff cannot anticipate needs and the organization cannot continue to meet its obligations.

Although talent cannot be assessed in dollars, like balance sheet tangibles, the current exposure level and potential risk can be predicted by simple analysis.

How are you currently evaluating your talent value?

Although financial reports use standard accounting methods to calculate dollar amounts for tangibles, assessing human resources requires less traditional metrics. One simple strategy to estimate an organization's current talent is to use the same P&L assessment tool called *Assets and Liabilities Ratio*. This methodology can be adapted to calculate line items to assess whether the current human resources situation is positive or negative. The McKinsey (2001) data offer compelling evidence that, "Companies [which look beyond the level of individual performance differentials to] recognize the strategic importance of talent and manage their businesses accordingly stand to reap very large rewards." The stability of a corporation's human assets directly affects its ability to build profitability over the long-term. An example of a tool that can be used is the Retention Risk Measure on page 13, which provides a framework example of how an organization can quantify the ratio of human resources assets to liabilities. As with a traditional balance sheet, the goal is to achieve the highest possible positive number in the total assets column.

Historically, employers had people lining up for open positions, but due to the change in population demographic employers must now compete aggressively both to sign new talent and to retain great employees. As a result, human resource costs (e.g., recruiting, sign-on bonuses, training, mentoring, and benefits) continue to rise significantly each year.

Leaders who regard these line items as investments rather than expenses are increasing the opportunities for retaining valuable talent. A couple of benefits:

- Each year an employee stays it offsets expensive replacement costs.

- Each year, the potential return on investment in a human resource grows exponentially as knowledge and experience are added. Two primary measures of performance are high productivity and quality that depend on employees being motivated on a daily basis and staying long enough to learn how to become an effective performer.

Talent Management Case Study

Underestimating the value of talent is a common mistake by leaders until they discover they have lost it.

A manufacturing company with $20 million in revenue returned a modest dividend of $2 million last year. The corporate financials, current market share, competition, trends, and technology convinced a potential buyer that the company was a good investment with high profit potential. Well, so the numbers said!

On his way to a final visit with the leadership and change management team on the day before the closing, the potential buyer was waiting for an elevator and struck up a conversation with a 29-year veteran of the company, who commented on how things were going to be changing soon. Surprised that someone might know about the highly confidential deal, the potential buyer asked, "What do you mean?" The employee shared widespread rumors about the company being sold and revealed that seven of the nine engineers would be eligible for full retirement in less than two years, leaving most critical positions empty and the result being over 210 years of collective industry experience walking out of the factory.

With no successors in place and an average learning curve of four to five years to get to the level of experience needed for this industry, the employee also speculated that the company's unique culture would make it difficult to find replacements who would stay around long enough to learn what they needed. He ended with a smile and the question, "So what about you, what brings you here today?"

How do you think the potential buyer's valuation of the company and his negotiating position were influenced by this two-minute conversation, if he found out this was true?

The point of this case study is organizations need talent because businesses are made of people. So what is your company doing to attract and retain talent?

Howatt HR Attraction and Retention Survey		
Answer true or false to the following 10 statements.		
Statements	**T**	**F**
1. I know how to calculate the costs of turnover in my company.		
2. I know what our attraction strategy is.		
3. I know what our retention strategy is.		
4. I know why people stay with our organization.		
5. I know why employees are attracted to our company.		
6. I know why people leave our organization.		
7. I know what the average turnover rate is in this industry.		
8. Our organization turnover rate is below industry standards.		
9. Our organization has made a commitment to become an employer of choice.		
10. Pay and rewards are clearly linked to performance in our organization.		
11. Our organization is committed to organizational learning.		
12. Our organization trains managers to select, on-board, coach, recognize, and reward good work with the goal of retaining quality workers.		
Totals		
If you answered four or more as being false there is an opportunity to improve your ability to retain your most valuable resource: your quality employees.		

The remainder of this book provides research, strategies, and tools for corporate leaders to consider as they begin to facilitate strategies that are effective at attracting and retaining talent. Though attraction and retention are important, so is having an engaged and motivated workforce. A lofty goal but a worthwhile one is to become an employer of choice. In chapter two, I will introduce a theory for examining the core elements for becoming an employer of choice.

Talent no longer refers to "innate ability," but is a new management buzzword used to refer to "brainpower" (either natural or trained), and is used by some to refer to their entire workforce and others to refer to the management of specific competencies. The bottom line is, however it is defined—there is a TALENT SHORTAGE looming. —The Economist

Retention Risk Measure

This tool assists in assessing workforce retention and associated risks. Based on your perceptions and experience, rate each of the items in the two columns below on a scale of 1 (low) to 5 (high). Add each column and then subtract the liabilities from the assets to approximate your current talent capacity presently being retained.

Assets		Liabilities	
Top executive(s) (CEO/Board of Directors) effectiveness		Confusion regarding authority and/or responsibilities	
Leadership effectiveness		High turnover	
Management strategy effectiveness		High absenteeism (average sick/missed days) vis a vis competitors	
Team building		Unmotivated workforce	
Highly Skilled Employees		Distrust of organization/leaders	
Employee loyalty		Misperceptions about corporate vision	
Organizational succession plan		Conflict among employees	
Professional development		Miscommunication	
Recruiting strategy		Dissatisfaction with job	
Knowledge management program		Undeveloped workers	
Positive corporate culture		Poor knowledge transfer	
Employee work ethic		At-risk behavior (addictions/violence)	
Performance management model		No standard performance measures	
Coaching and mentoring		Noncompliance issues	
Regular feedback		Under-utilized resources	
Career planning		Perception of favoritism	
Recognition program		Employee opinions not solicited	
Positive role models		Lateness (to work and/or meetings)	
Ethics and professionalism		Dissent among managers/leaders	
Employee pride		Disrespect for diversity	
TOTAL ASSETS		**TOTAL LIABILITIES**	

Retention Risk Quick Ratio

Use the totals above in the formula below. As with traditional methods, a result of 1 is satisfactory. Less than 1 signals potential retention risk problems.

Total Assets: ____ ÷ Total Liabilities: ____ = Quick Ratio: ____

CHAPTER 2

Triangulation Theory

The demographic shortfall that is currently happening will make the talent war of the late 1990s seem like a minor irritation. —Anthony Carnevale, Former Chairman of the National Commission for Employment Policy

A topic that continues to gain popularity and concern in corporate boardrooms is the challenge of attracting and retaining the right employees. For years, a commonly used phrase, "our most valuable resource is our employee," was espoused by corporate leaders. Too often this verbiage was, under examination, nothing more than lip service because corporate leaders were not fully engaged in developing a comprehensive strategy for attracting and retaining the right talent. But today things are changing. One of the greatest challenges in terms of talent management is attracting and getting the right talent in the right place, and then figuring out how to keep the talent motivated and committed to an organization (Fieldglass, 2008).

Today is different; corporate leaders who want to stay competitive know that good talent is a natural resource like oil. There is only so much and it can't be wasted, because once it's gone it's gone. Conservation of good talent is a critical paradigm that's becoming more difficult due to the aging population demographic. One of the core agitators for the current talent management crisis in North America is the growing talent shortage. Western Compensation & Benefits Consultants (2007), in a survey conducted with 446 organizations across Canada, reported from the sampled population 87% were experiencing difficulty attracting employees and 66% reported concerns with retention.

The fact is, attraction and retention are becoming more complex because as the labor pool reduces it is harder to attract new talent. According to a 2007 Manpower study of 37,000 employers in 27 countries, 41% of companies worldwide are having difficulty filling positions due to a lack of suitable talent. And when research from Taleo Research (2007) suggests that regardless of the economy companies can expect to rehire between 20% and 25% of their company workforce, it's becoming critically important for companies to take as much action as possible, regardless of the economy, to drive down this attrition rate. The researcher also reported that an Accenture survey of more than 850 top executives from around the globe reported that attracting and retaining top talent for a company's success is second only to competition.

Employee job satisfaction can be directly impacted by attraction and retention of a workforce (Griffeth, Hom, & Gaertner, 2000). When employees are not satisfied with their company's behavior, the company is at risk of losing them (Mossholder, Settoon, & Henagan, 2005). Cascio (2003) reports that direct turnover costs run between 1.5 and 2.5 times the annual salary of an employee. Best-selling author Brandon Scott (2005), in *Top Grading*, suggests replacing top talent in organizations often ends up costing companies a mind-blowing 15 times the employee's salary. His assumptions are based in his research around the associated costs of not getting the right person in the right position. On average, corporations spend 36% of their revenue on human capital expenses. Assuming an average rate of employee turnover of 25% and a cost associated with turnover equivalent to salary, the cost of turnover represents about 9% of revenue (Lermusiaux, 2005). The author goes to provide an example of the cost of turnover and the incentive for reducing turnover: in a company with 100,000 employees at an average salary of $40,000, a 10% turnover rate costs $400 million. A turnover reduction of one-half percent would result in savings of $2 million.

In addition to attracting and retaining talent, an IMB human capital study (2008) that involved more than 400 human resource senior executives reported that more than 75% of organizations are now reporting a projected shortfall in the pool of future leaders. The research unpacks the challenge that a company's ability to attract qualified candidates, align employee skills with organizational needs, rapidly adjust to change, and develop new skills in leadership and workforce are stressing corporate leaders in retaining a competent and skilled workforce. A recent Conference Board survey reported that limited career opportunities was found to be the number one drive of overall employee dissatisfaction, cited by 59% of respondents.

Gleebbeek and Bax (2004) report that reducing the cost of turnover of quality employees is big business; for example, reducing the turnover of quality employees by one per month will save $360,000 a year for a $20,000 job and $720,000 for a $40,000 job. Regardless of the costs in dollars and cents for replacing talent, the mental brain units of managers' time, loss of productivity, and loss of critical institutional knowledge are additional costs that have a negative impact on an organization's bottom line.

Branham's Top 8 Reasons Why Good Employees Leave (2001):

- There is no direct link between their pay and their performance.

- They do not see a clear path for growth and career advancement.

- They do not perceive from the organizational leadership that their work is important.

- They do not believe they are being recognized for the work they are doing.

- They do not get to use their natural strengths and talents.

- They have unclear or even unrealistic expectations that were not calibrated in the interview process.

- They will no longer stand for abusive managers.

- They will no longer work in a toxic work environment.

The balance of this chapter introduces a theory on attraction and retention that provides a framework of what and how an organization can put itself into a position to become an employer of choice.

Becoming an Employer of Choice

An employer of choice by definition is an organization that employees want to work for because it has proven itself as being concerned and motivated to influence the following three elements: job satisfaction, culture, and organization maturity. At this point of evolution, an organization has positioned itself to achieve what ultimately brands employers in its industry. The distinction of becoming an employer of choice is critical for facilitating employee engagement that synergistically facilitates the above three elements. A 2002 Gallup survey reported that less than a quarter of American workers are fully "engaged" in their work, costing the US economy $300 billion. Curt Coffman and Gabriel Gonzalez-Mobina (2002) add the following compelling research points:

The cost of disengaged workers to the United States economy is estimated between $254 billion and $363 billion annually. One of the single biggest signs of disengagement is absenteeism and in the United States it is estimated to be costing employers $40 billion per year.

Hundreds of Gallup polls have reported that organizations that are able to engage their workforce are able to out-perform companies that have not, for example: 86% higher customer service ratings, 70% more success in lowering turnover rates, 70% higher productivity, 44% more profitability and 78% better safety records.

The point being, attracting and retaining employees are important, but perhaps more important are the engagement and commitment of the workforce that have a direct impact on an organization's ability to achieve its business maturity. "What we're hearing is that people want to contribute more. But they say their leaders and supervisors unintentionally put obstacles in their paths," said Donald Lowman, a Managing Director of Towers Perrin HR Services Business (Amble, 2005).

The Triangulation Theory focuses on facilitating a framework for attracting candidates, retaining top talent, and motivating and engaging a workforce.

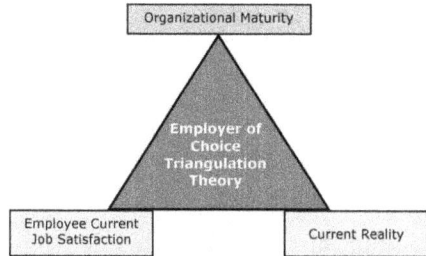

The Hewitt Top 50 Employers in Canada Survey's core criterion for evaluating an Employer of Choice is the degree of employee emotional and intellectual commitment demonstrated by the workforce. Schneider, Gruman, and Coutts (2005) explain a helpful science called social psychology is a proven methodology for discovering the interconnection between how people think and feel influences and motivates behavior. To achieve this shift in a workforce organization evolution and to create the change needed in a workforce, it is important to be aware that the power of emotions and thoughts of each individual collectively create the whole and the power of group think in influencing organizational change. Members of the group build consensus, using a structured process to share thinking. "Group think" is often derided in our culture; credible corporate leaders allow cognitive dissonance to enter their leadership style. Cognitive dissonance is the psychological state that facilitates an uncomfortable internal ambivalence between what one promotes to the world as being true and what one knows to be true. To become an employer of choice, leaders must not avoid the truth; they need to welcome it, take on the challenge, and be committed to action.

There are large financial incentives to committing to the process of becoming an employer of choice (where top talent wants to be). Superior business productivity and increased profits are directly correlated to superior talent (Michaels, Handfield-Jones, & Axelrod, 2001). These authors' landmark book, *War On Talent,* provided evidence of the strategic advantage for attracting and retaining top talent in an organization.

Up to the 1980s, a company typically was worth about the same as its book value; however, in the 1980s, the stock market began to show that the market values of some companies were increasing faster than their book values. According to research by Baruch Lev, by 2000 the average S&P 500 company had a market value six times higher than book value. This shows that a company's value cannot be found solely on a balance sheet; it's found in intangibles. Another recent study, by Sirota Survey Intelligence, found that the stock prices of 11 high-morale companies increased an average of 19.4%, outpacing their competitors' 8% rise. A 2005 Watson Wyatt study indicated that companies with highly engaged employees typically achieve a financial performance *four times better* than companies with poor employee attitudes.

Two global benchmarks that help an organization evaluate its progression towards or away from being an employer of choice: 1) attraction, 2) retention. When employees want to work for and stay with an organization, these two results will, over time, manifest and facilitate social attitudes and perceptions of people both internal and external to the company of the value and benefits for working for it. This helps companies leverage the power of group think to their advantage.

Unfortunately, some organizations think becoming an employer of choice is basically an activity that helps promote and position the corporate brand. This is a fallacy. This accomplishment will occur only through intention and action to facilitate targeted behaviors for influencing an organization's workforce's emotions and thinking. Ask any Olympic athlete, "How did you win a gold medal?" Their answer will be something like, "By focusing on becoming the best, one day at a time, day in and day out, for the past four years." Nothing is done overnight. Success cannot be bought; it is earned.

Being an employer of choice is about much more than external awards. Malcolm Gladwell (2002), author of *The Tipping Point: How Little Things Can Make a Big Difference,* explains the phenomenon of word of mouth in reference to how it is a natural part of every employee's life.

All of these little conversations employees have with each other define and facilitate the kind of branding epidemic organizational leaders are looking for. Although, employees sharing their messages about what it's like to work for a company will spread through a community and plant like viruses. A critical insight from Gladwell is the judgment from the workforce's perspective—good or bad—will determine how successful an organization's quest for becoming an employer of choice will be. Again, the metrics of attraction and retention will serve as a beacon if the organization is moving in the right direction.

Organizations that are committed to becoming an employer of choice understand that when new employees start a role, the majority bring their dreams and energy (head, heart, and hand). Employers that don't get this quickly quell this new enthusiasm and end up with an employee only willing to bring their hands to work, and too often speak with their feet. Frederick Reichheld (2001), author of *The Loyalty Effect,* reports in organizations where the leadership is committed to both its employees and customers in a statement directed to the workforce: "I believe this organization deserves my loyalty," 70% to 80% of employees responded the company deserved their loyalty. The author goes on to explain in these kinds of companies employee attraction and retention metrics were more favorable than their competitors. The family-owned billion-dollar business enterprise's simple vision: take care of their staff and customers first and the profits will take care of themselves (Kazanjian, 2007). This commitment has led to impressive attraction and retention data when compared to its competitors and to market share and profitability.

Measuring Attraction

The talent pool is simply not as vast as it once was. The days of putting an ad in the paper and getting hundreds of motivated and highly skilled employees are gone. When a job becomes vacant, human resource departments often track a couple of core stats to evaluate the abundance of the talent pool, using yield ratios, and the percentage of applicants that proceeds to the next stage of the selection process: 1) Lead generation ratio compares candidates invited for interviews to the number of candidates interviewed, compared to number of offers made to number of new hires; compared to number of new hires that after year one are considered good hires and are fitting well into the organization; 2) Lead time average: amount of time it takes to find and get a person through the selection process to hiring and on-boarding; 3) Selection ratio: number of applicants hired divided by the number of total applicants. The goal is to keep this number as high as possible (e.g., 1:2 ratio would be low).

The average time required to replace an employee over the past several years has risen from 41 to 51 days, which significantly raises recruiting costs and lowers productivity (Clark, 1999). Branham (2001) provides an example of a protocol that outlines factors for consideration when studying attraction rates:

- Percentage of application considered "A" candidates.

- Average number of days to fill vacancy.

- Application dropout rate.

- Number of recruiting sources used.

- Percentile rank of total compensation versus talent competitors.

- Percentage of new hire referrals who stay at least six months.

- Average monthly percentage of open positions.

Employers are starting to discover that the days of being the institution with all the power are gone. This was referred to as an employers' market. Today, it's more of an employees' market, meaning top talent can be more selective and can have greater expectations and demands for employers. This is happening because the majority of companies across North America that require highly skilled talent are finding this talent pool is getting older and the replacement pool is shrinking. Employers don't have the luxury of burning through employees, knowing more will come.

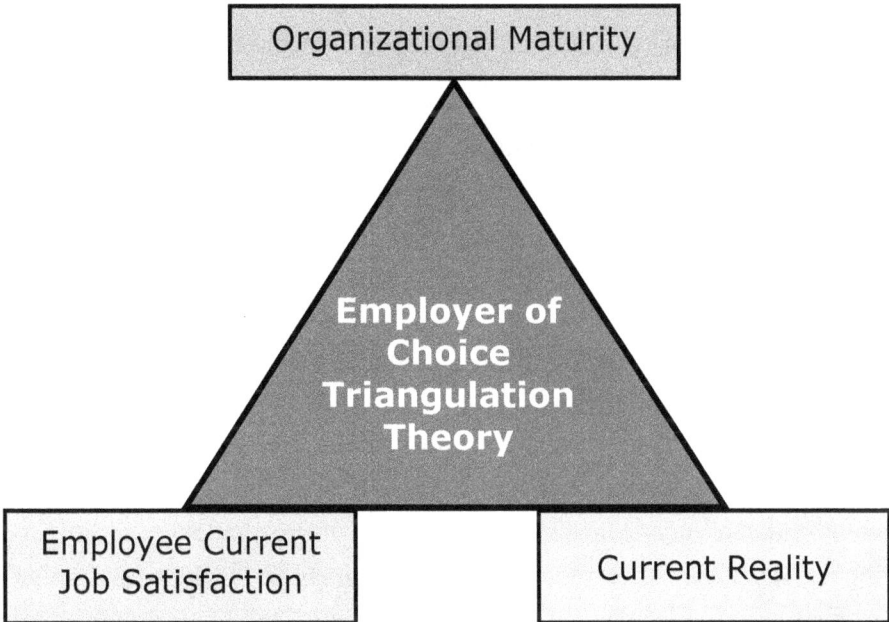

Figure 1—Employer of Choice Triangulation Theory

Employer of Choice Triangulation Theory

Employer of Choice Triangulation Theory is a strategic organizational learning theory that provides a frame of reference for understanding how to become an employer of choice. It also diagnoses the strategies and actions an employer can take to improve attraction and retention.

The core hypothesis of this theory is to become an employer of choice an organization must be in position to attract and retain a motivated and engaged workforce. Accomplishing this provides an opportunity for an organization to achieve its full financial potential.

Employee of Choice Triangulation Theory has three core elements. The model is called a Triangulation Theory because any of the three points can directly impact any of the other two positively or negatively in reference to influencing organizational performance. Each element has performance behaviors that influence an organization's success in a particular element:

- The majority of individuals within the workforce must perceive individual job satisfaction.

- The organizational culture must be congruent and committed and demonstrate actions needed to achieve the organization's core value and business goals.

- The organization must achieve organizational maturity.

Consider the example of an organization where the majority of employees do not feel a sense of job satisfaction. This can negatively influence the organization's culture. In this example, the organization's attraction and retention numbers, when benchmarked against its competitors, could indicate higher levels of turnover and more challenges in attracting the right kind of employees than its competitors. If the organization wanted to influence change based on this theory, the first step would be to look at the behaviors it could stop and those it could start that would assist in influencing employee job satisfaction.

There may be no better evidence of the value of this theory in action than studying the leadership strategy of Jack Welch. He positioned GE as one of the most iconic corporations in the world. He focused on specific behaviors he believed were needed for an organization in reference to people, process, and product. Slater (1999) reported that Welch focused on ensuring leaders in the company followed the company's values, were held accountable, focused on developing a learning organization that empowered its workforce, and held the course that a commitment to grow and change would be a core imperative that would define the organization's success. The result of this strategy was GE had no problem attracting or retaining top talent. In essence, it evolved into the quintessential employer of choice.

Elements for Organizational Maturity

The output of organizational maturity is an organization has matured to the point it is on track to achieve its full potential. Six important measures that influence the organization's potential capacity are the six

Ps: *people, processes, policies, projections, productivity, and profitability.* The results in each of these six Ps will ultimately determine the organization's success and value. Peter Senge (1990) taught for an organization to evolve to its full potential it must educate its workforce to give up traditional ways of thinking, develop core competencies, learn to embrace change, accept that organization success depends on the behaviours of many, and get the workforce to buy into an ambitious vision.

Below are core behaviors that influence an organization's capacity to achieve organizational maturity. Each of the behaviors would need to evaluated and assessed to determine the current level of effectiveness of each and whether each is facilitating behaviors to improve attraction and retention. To measure organizational maturity an organization can compare the perceptions of its leadership, stakeholders, employees, and customers to discern how these perceptions are influencing the other two elements.

Defined Employee Value Proposition—Every organization consciously or unconsciously defines its employee value proposition by its actions. The employee value proposition answers the "why" question in reference to why employees would want to come and stay with an organization. Corporate Leadership Counsel (2007) states the top two attractors as to why employees come to a company are competitive compensation packages and organizational stability; however, the top three reasons they stay are senior management, management effectiveness, and collegial workplace. Both attraction and retention strategies are integrated into the organization's employee value proposition. It's critical to not only develop an employee value proposition but also to communicate it and monitor and measure it to ensure it's a catalyst for attraction and retention. If not, change it.

Executive Leadership Capacity—Perhaps one of the single biggest reasons organizations fail to achieve their full potential is poor executive leadership. In a competitive global economy, an organization without visionary executive leadership often fails to reap the benefits of attracting and retaining a motivated workforce because leadership has taken a narrow view and is focused only on near-term profits. Tietjen and Myers' (1998) research found that leadership style has a direct impact on influencing employee satisfaction. Effective executive leadership drives the six Ps through strategic and critical thinking, strategic and business planning, defining management accountabilities and expectations at all levels, and following measuring and monitoring success. Collins (2001), author of *Good to Great,* reports the five core imperatives for organizational success are: competent employees, people working together, effective management, effective leadership, and effective executive leadership.

Supervisory Style—Schneider, Gruman, and Coutts (2005) explain the field of social psychology focuses on studying the correlation between how people think, feel, and relate to each other; and collectively how this influences human behavior. The authors go on to provide an historical example of one of the first great thinkers in this field, Kurt Lewin, who, in the 1930s, had an interest in how people, interpersonal relations, and productivity are impacted by supervisory style. Many people have left their jobs because of nothing other than an inability to have a productive and professional relationship with their direct supervisor. In addition, when employees and supervisors are in conflict the consequence can be hours of lost productivity and inefficiency. One of the core functions of effective supervisors is to facilitate the workplace environment.

Quality of Communications—Communication effectiveness (e.g., how effectively information is distributed) is critical for an organization to achieve its full potential. The accuracy and frequency of vertical and horizontal communication influences decision making that impacts the six Ps, as well as the workforce's group think. Bennis (1990) supports this observation and adds the organization's leadership communication needs to make sense and be sensitive to the receiver's needs and values. Communication is important, but so is the message. In the information age, the quality of communication can impact the culture as well as employee satisfaction. Information is king and when people don't know or worry they don't know they are left to their own perceptions, which may be wrong. Graham and Messner (1998) promote that quality of communication influences employee satisfaction. One kind of communication that detracts from organizational maturity is miscommunication. Miscommunication can cost organizations millions of dollars in immediate lost opportunity and productivity, and promote long-term damage by negatively conditioning corporate culture.

Performance Management—Motivating employees and developing talent to its full potential require a process where employees know they can learn and grow, as well as help ensure the right employees are in the right jobs. An effective performance management model aligns business and people. It begins in recruiting (hiring the people with the right competencies), on-boarding, meaningful performance review process, meaningful out-of-cycle feedback, meaningful professional development planning, and meaningful learning and growth opportunities. All of these are interconnected to assist each employee develop their core competencies that have been determined important to drive business success. In addition, workforce planning is important to monitor and measure workforce needs and talent capacity (e.g., one measure is average age for all critical positions), as well as the development of organizational succession planning. In 2000, the head of training for Motorola estimated that, "The company is getting $30 back for every dollar it spends on training its people. This is said to be the highest payoff investment of time and money that the company can make. Other companies report similar returns on their investment in training their executives and staff" (Tracy, 2000).

Commitment to Quality—W. Edwards Deming (1999), a statistician, taught business leaders how to be responsive to the demands of quality and efficiency. To instill this responsiveness, the workforce needed to have leadership that was interested in both motivating and empowering employees. The 'Deming model,' considered the grandfather of Total

Quality Management (TQM), had a major impact on leadership methodologies in the 1980s (Walton, 1986). The functional to organizational quality control is really a philosophy about how a company will do business (e.g., customer service expectations) and the measures of success. Organizations use quality control thinking to assist in the process for measuring and monitoring the behaviors needed for increasing both attraction and retention. Some examples of the kinds of metrics organizations are using to evaluate employee perceptions are surveys (e.g., engagement surveys, interviewing new hire surveys), focus groups, and exit interviews. The rationale of this activity is to help organizations understand whether they are making progress in attracting and retaining a motivated workforce. In addition, other quality control activities involve looking for best practices, internal and external benchmarking, and always looking for opportunities to make improvements.

Ability to Transfer Knowledge—Knowledge Management is the science of processing and capturing the available sum of knowledge that is useable throughout an organization. Information comprises the meaning given to data. This is known as explicit knowledge (Nonaka & Takeuchi, 1995). The knowledge components of culture and skills represent implicit knowledge, which depends on the individual and is stored in the minds of people. This concept is difficult to describe; is based on experience; and is practical in nature. Explicit knowledge, on the contrary, is not dependent on the individual; is theoretical in nature; and is specified as procedures, theories, equations, manuals, drawings, etc. This knowledge is mainly stored in management information, technical systems, and organizational routines. Organizational maturity is impacted by how effectively an organization can keep its workforce educated with the information it needs. An organization that retains its workforce provides perhaps one of the most important elements for organizational maturity: it has secured the critical institutional knowledge (tacit) that represents 80% of the knowledge needed to operate a business to its full potential.

Capacity to Manage Change—One constant all organizations can count on is change. Schein (1985) says leadership effectiveness plays a crucial role in determining the culture of an organization and the role of its change management program (e.g., communications programs, personnel issues, change management strategies, rewards management). How effective an organization is at managing change, facilitating change, and preparing its workforce for change have a direct influence on the heads, hearts, and minds of its workforce. Two events that are important to manage successfully when dealing with organizational change: 1) how the change will impact individuals, 2) how the change will help the business mature. Both are important questions that require clarity, strategic thinking, and preparation before implementing any change. Once a decision has been made to make a change, the organization must rely on the effectiveness of its change managing program to implement the change. How the organization manages change directly influences the culture and employees' confidence.

Elements that Define Cultural Reality

Cultural reality refers to how a culture (majority of the workforce) is behaving toward individuals internal and external to an organization. Corporate leaders who want to evolve their organization to its full potential understand that facades and illusion are not reality. What the corporate culture believes, feels, and does defines it. No marketing campaign can cover deep wounds.

It's critical for corporate leadership to not only give lip service to the importance of the corporate culture but to spend time understanding how this powerful intangible influences employee attitudes and behaviors. Appreciative inquiry is based in the social sciences and provides a frame of reference for understanding, changing, and enhancing corporate cultures. Appreciative inquiry ". . . refers to both a search for knowledge and a theory of intentional collective action, which are designed to help evolve the normative vision and will of a group, organization, or society as a whole" (Cooperrider & Srivastva,

1987). This theory teaches that making a commitment to evolve and improve the corporate culture is not just about focusing on what's not working; it's also about improving what's working well and building on it.

Below are core perceptions and behaviors that influence an organization's capacity to achieve its defined cultural reality. Each of the behaviors must be evaluated for corporate leaders to make an accurate assessment of the current level of cultural reality and the strengths and benefits of the culture for attraction and retention:

Money vs. Meaningful Work. It's true that money has been found to be the number one motivator for attracting new employees. However, Ken Blanchard and Sheldon Bowles (1998), authors of *Gung Ho!,* teach that employees rarely stay with an organization just for money; they stay in organizations where they perceive they are doing meaningful work. This occurs when employees understand the value of their role to an organization's success. Employees who stay for just a paycheque often are average to under-performers. For an organization to achieve its full potential it needs people who are passionate, committed, and skilled. In addition to getting paid, being acknowledged for good work is important for employees. Recognition and rewards programs help facilitate and teach leaders how to reward good behavior to show the workforce is not just about doing your job; it's about doing it well. These programs go beyond paycheques as they help to show employees the organization values and needs their best contributions. When employees feel a sense of meaning from their work it influences job satisfaction, corporate productivity, and profits. However, keep in mind compensation is important and it must always be competitive, fair (there is a clear link between performance and pay), and balanced with meaningful work.

Corporate Values vs. Assumptions. Many corporations have taken the time to create a set of corporate values, package them nicely, and even post them on the walls. The realism between the publicly presented corporate values and employee assumptions directly defines the current cultural reality. In essence, the congruency between what executives say and do determines what the workforce believes and this determines the overall morale level of the majority of the workforce. For example, if the values say something like, "We care for our employees...," and no one talks to the employees, this behavior is incongruent with the message. The result is some employees may feel like no one cares about them and this can contribute to workplace stress, which is a major issue and perhaps one of the most costly realities that is growing. The *APA Monitor* (2008) reported that 75% of Americans mentioned that work is a major stress and, in fact, 48% believe their stress has increased over the last year. When an organization states it cares but the majority of the workforce believes it doesn't do enough and cares only about profits, this generates a gap between the corporate line and cultural reality that negatively influences the attitudes and behavior of employees. Another example of a stressor is when corporate leaders say all employees are treated equally, but only the senior leaders get the perks. What message does this send?

Respect vs. Lack of Trust. Respect is demonstrated in behaviors such as active listening and appreciating another person's point of view. Lack of trust is demonstrated when an employer says they will do something for an employee and never follows through. Lying to employees is perhaps the fastest way a leader can lose respect. Employers who engage a workforce without a keen understanding of the importance of building respectful and trusting workplaces will never get the hearts and heads of its workforce; only its hands. The degree of respect and trust in organizations is directly related to the amount of conflict in a culture. Conflict is expensive, unproductive, and negatively influences both employee job satisfaction and organizational maturity. From a behavioral science perspective, it's often impossible to get the entire workforce to respect and trust the organization's intentions because of personalities and values differences; however, the majority of the workforce will define the cultural reality.

Organizational Co-operation. Organizations are made up of people and when people within an organization can work together on supportive and caring teams this collaboration and co-operation directly benefit corporate profitability, because more tasks get done when people work together toward a common set of goals. However, cooperation takes energy and effort. A high level of reciprocity ensures that the benefits of cooperation exceed the costs. Based on the reciprocity principle, most employees starting a new role expect their good turns to be returned. A benevolent act (e.g., giving a person a lift to or from work, covering a temporary absence, giving someone advance notice of an event, etc.) carries implicit price tags and is paid in intangible currencies like those listed above. If the recipient of a good deed is in a position to return a favor and does not, they are a defector. This lack of response undermines cooperation and often is perceived as a relationship breach. The consequence usually is an embargo is placed on doing future good turns for a defector. When an organization doesn't work together cooperatively, with the root cause being a lack of adherence to the reciprocity principle, there is wasted energy (e.g., complaining, criticism, and resentment) that impacts job satisfaction and organizational maturity. Team building is, in essence, a strategy for reducing defectors.

Organizational Commitment. Cultures where the majority of the workforce is proud of the organization can have a profound impact on defining the organization's work ethic. When the majority of the workforce believes in what they are doing, this level of commitment facilitates discretionary effort (the degree of energy employees will exert in the workplace) that influences other employees (Catlette, 2000). Every employee has about 15%-25% capacity that is left to their discretion whether they will put it forth or not. Organizations that can tap into this additional effort have in essence multiplied their workforce without adding new head count. Consider if you had 100 employees who all brought 15% more effort to the job willingly (head and heart); this would be like having an additional 15 employees. A workforce that's tapping into its discretionary effort is evidence it's committed to the organization.

Level of Fear. Dr. Deming also studied the impact of the work culture and how it affects productivity and quality. In *The New Economics* (1994) he reported that performance of the workforce is influenced and governed largely by the system (e.g., management model). In his book, *Out of the Crisis,* (2000) he argued that negative psychological forces such as fear actually impeded progress and lowered productivity. In cultures where employees are fearful, they have an adverse impact on job satisfaction and organizational maturity. The challenge with fear is that it can be as damaging being perceived as real. It's critical for leaders to be aware of culture perceptions and to drive fear out of an organization, as it will only force compliance; it never promotes or develops competencies that are needed for an organization to evolve and grow to its full potential. Managers who use fear and get what they think are results are blind to how better their results could be with another approach.

Open to Generational Differences. Generational differences are influenced by society; chronology is a by-product. Different age groups' values have been influenced and often shaped by the world events of their time. For this reason, a leader may need to look beyond a person's chronological age to accurately understand what this generation has learned and how these learnings influence their motivation. As mentioned earlier, there are four different generation groups: Traditionalists, Baby Boomers, Generation X, and Generation Y, all with their own set of values, views, and beliefs. When looking at evolving a culture it's important to understand the needs for the entire workforce and to build strategies and ways of doing business that are flexible enough to help all employees, regardless of their generation, have an opportunity to meet their needs in the workplace. No one generation can be viewed as more important than another; each one has value and something to offer the workplace. For example, a traditionalist has tacit knowledge that the generation Yer will need to build the organization's future.

Performance Evaluation Attitudes. How a culture evaluates performance can influence attitudes. Baron, Byrne, and Branscombe (2006) report a common mistake that can negatively influence attitude when evaluating performance are fundamental attribution errors (FAE). In essence, FAE attributes the cause of an issue more to the person (who is the attention of focus) than the possibility of external causes to make evaluations about the person's character or capacity (Jones & Harris, 1967). An example is when an onlooker who is evaluating gaps makes the assumption that the gap is due to some personal characteristics (e.g., lazy) rather than considering the possibility some external cause may be influencing the behavior. Cultures can be conditioned by attitudes and perception. When employees feel they are being evaluated fairly and expectations are realistic this promotes a culture of trust and respect that facilitates open communication. Corporate leaders need to ensure the US vs. THEM thinking does not blossom in the culture. This is created by having one set of rules for managers and another for employees. This mindset in a culture influences how managers evaluate employees and how employees evaluate managers. This performance evaluation attitude directly influences the culture and the games people play that can influence performance.

Corporate Brand in the Marketplace. Ambler and Barrow (1996) first defined employee branding as the functional, economic, and psychological benefits package employers were willing to provide their employees. Minchington (2005) explains corporate brand is how an organization is viewed by the marketplace in reference to being a great place to work or not. This brand influences how people feel about the organization they work in. Organizations that pay attention to the corporate brand understand the direct relationship between attracting and retaining employees. Brands are earned. The employer branding process is about building and sustaining employment propositions that are compelling and different and alive in the minds of employees. Corporate leaders must keep a close eye on their brand and its influence on attraction and retention of its workforce, and, yes, profit.

Elements that Define Employee Job Satisfaction

Based on a study of over 5,000 households, the United States Conference Board (2007) reported less than half of all Americans interviewed said they were satisfied with their jobs, down from 61% 20 years ago. McClelland (1988) determined that each employee has the following three needs: 1) need for achievement (i.e., to be successful); 2) need for power (i.e., to have choice); and 3) need for affiliation (i.e., to feel connected). How employees believe their needs are being met in the workplace influences the group think of the culture. Job satisfaction can be directly influenced by the corporate culture and organization maturity elements.

Mayo oversaw research from 1924 to 1927 at Western Electric in Chicago, where he uncovered what he called the Hawthorne Effect, a set of conditions that motivated employees. One of his most impressive findings was that all employees have a profound need for recognition, security, and a sense of belonging. One of the most effective ways to motivate an employee "…is listening to employees, introduce them to their new companions, and get them congenial work associates" (Mayo, 1945). The author goes on to suggest when this happens building teams takes less work, effort, time, and commitment.

Below are core perceptions and behaviors that influence employee attitudes in regard to job satisfaction. To obtain the employees' point of view, engage them directly and engage a large enough sample to ensure the data have achieved the needed statistical level of confidence in regard to both validity (determines if a measure does what it is supposed to) and reliability (refers to consistency of a measure).

Frederick Herzberg's two-factor, or motivation-hygiene, theory looks at what an employer can do to increase satisfaction and decrease dissatisfaction, such as improving the job environment, which includes: policies, procedures, supervision, and working conditions (Herzberg, Mausner, & Snyderman, 1959). Herzberg's (1982) research began with a methodology that resulted in interviewing over 200 engineers and accountants, using a critical incident method to collect data. The results led to the development of two continuums (satisfaction and decrease dissatisfaction) that were found to be independent of each other but influenced employee job satisfaction attitude in regard to whether the workplace was good or bad.

Based on the research of Herzberg's (1968) two-factor theory, people are influenced by two factors: 1) Satisfaction and psychological growth are a result of 'motivation factors'; 2) Dissatisfaction is a result of a lack of 'hygiene factors.' He suggested in the workplace human beings have two basic needs: to avoid pain and to grow psychologically. He believed money as a motivator to keep employees over the long term is quite low; in the end, people need to be interested in what they do. And if they do stay around for money, they are not going to perform to their full potential, as this will not be enough of a motivator.

To understand employee job satisfaction, employers need to understand how the majority of employees perceive and think about each of the following elements:

Hygiene factors are important, as they help prevent employees from getting discouraged. Keep in mind that the factors listed below are based on an employee's motivation and ability to learn how to meet their intrinsic needs through their work. The typical factor an employee evaluates to determine if they feel a sense of job satisfaction is the level of success they can achieve in each of the below areas. The typical factors are:

- *Personal achievement*—e.g., the degree an employee feels an internal sense of accomplishment for achieving their daily goals.

- *Responsibility for tasks*—e.g., the amount of pride and ownership for assigned tasks and commitment to completing them in a timely manner.

- *Interest in job*—e.g., level at which an employee gets up each day to go to work.

- *Advancement to higher level tasks*—e.g., the amount an employee believes they have the potential to grow.

- *Recognition for achievement*—e.g., sense of accomplishment an employee has for knowing they are doing a good job without external recognition.

- *Personal growth*—e.g., the confidence an employee has that their current role is assisting in their personal growth.

- *Career path*—e.g., the clarity an employee has of the career path opportunities and the knowledge of what they must do to advance and grow.

Most recognition and reward programs are based around the idea of doing for an employee so that they feel valued and are more likely to want to come to work for a company, as well as to stay. However, though the below motivation factors are important there is no more important strategy than getting employees to learn how to operate from an internal locus of control. Dr. William Glasser, author of *Choice Theory*, teaches each person will ultimately have to take responsibility to learn how to meet their own needs for their personal happiness and fulfillment. He adds that many people don't know how to meet their needs, but they can be taught how to. So any employer of choice program needs to keep in mind it's not just an activity of doing *for*, it's an activity of doing *with* as well (e.g., teaching employees how to balance work and home life issues to reduce addictive disorders, how to deal with relationship and work related issues, or learn how to set and achieve goals).

Motivational factors are needed to motivate and influence the workforce. The typical factors are:

- *Working conditions*—e.g., cleanliness, organization, equipment, ergonomics, quality of air, noise, smell, schedule.

- *Quality of supervision*—e.g., professionalism, style, commitment, expertise, leadership ability, decision making, approachability.

- *Compensation package*—e.g., salary, benefits, incentive programs, overtime, retirement packages, leave opportunities.

- *Employment status*—e.g., full-time, part-time, flexibility.

- *Job security*—e.g., stable employer, stable economy, stable industry.

- *Company*—e.g., brand of company to the workforce—current and future.

- *Job function*—e.g., clearly defined role, responsibility, account-abilities, reporting structure, criteria used to measure success.

- *Company politics*—e.g., degree of obvious favoritism, application of rules, level of equity for all, leadership adherence to rules, stance, and actions on workforce bullying.

- *Interpersonal relationships*—e.g., how people treat each other, what leadership allows and does not allow.

There is a process a person goes through that influences both their emotions and thinking and ultimately drives their behavior and choices. Each employee keeps score of how they believe they are being treated and whether the work environment is meeting their expectation. For example, Herzberg (1968) reported the relationship an employee had with their supervisor and the quality of the interpersonal interaction were critical variables in predicting overall job satisfaction. Retaining employees who are not engaged can be as costly as turning over employees. This is why employee engagement is a reality employers are starting to come to learn is important. However, too often managers are too slow to respond to and understand what has gone wrong, and in many cases are too late to offer a better way once they discover the problems. What triggers the 13-step process can vary, such as: being passed over for a promotion, realizing that what was promised is not going to happen, change in role without a discussion, discovering unethical behavior, and observing racism and discrimination.

Thirteen Steps

1. Start a new job with enthusiasm

2. Question the decision to accept the job.

3. Think seriously about quitting.

4. Try to change things.

5. Resolve to quit.

6. Consider the cost of quitting.

7. Passively seek another job.

8. Prepare to actively seek another job.

9. Actively seek another job.

10. Get new job offer.

11. Quit, accept new job, or

12. Quit without a new job.

13. Stay and be disengaged.

What is important for employers to know is there are actions they can take that will assist in keeping employees satisfied and reduce the risk of their becoming dissatisfied. This is needed to assist the culture to transform into the kind of culture the organization wants and needs as in the end an organization will be only as good as its people.

Putting Theory Into Action

The purpose of this theory is to provide a framework to understand core elements that require attention for an employer to increase its ability to attract and retain top talent. The metaphor of employer of choice is powerful, as it represents an attractive destination for any organization. The three-step model below provides a strategy for taking the Triangulation Theory from concept to action.

Step 1—Defining Organizational Expectations. The first step to put this theory into action is to discover executive leadership expectations and degree of commitment to them. To make the changes need and to put this theory into action the leadership must be fully engaged.

   This theory provides a framework for recognizing the critical behaviors that influence a company's capacity to attract and retain the right talent. However, for this theory to work in any organization it must be aligned to the executive leadership strategic plan around attraction, retention, and profitability, as this drives the level of commitment and action the organization puts forward.

The following questions are to be answered by the executive leadership to ensure leaders are committed and motivated to facilitate the work that must be done to become an employer of choice.

- What does being an employer of choice mean?

- Why is it important to the business to become an employer of choice?

- Does the senior leadership agree with the thesis outlined by this theory?

- What resource will the senior leadership deploy to achieve this goal of becoming an employer of choice?

- What metrics will the senior leadership use to evaluate success (e.g., retention numbers, employee engagement survey, and decrease in sick time)?

The answers to these questions form the benchmark and expectations of the executive leadership. The next step is to determine through a gap analysis how aligned the organization is to the current expectation of the executive leadership. As well, senior leadership must examine in more depth what measures and metrics it wants to use to understand how big the gap is and the amount of commitment and effort it will take to move the organization in the direction it needs to go to achieve the desired results.

Step 2—*Gap Analysis.* To get to this point the executive leadership have fully endorsed and in fact has asked for a process that will facilitate the accurate discovery and assessment as to how the organization is currently performing in all the elements that make up job satisfaction, cultural reality, and organizational maturity. The thesis being, if the organization is under-performing in any of the elements it will not achieve its potential for attraction, retention, and profitability.

Triangulation Theory analysis requires an understanding of how the organization is performing in each of the three core elements of job satisfaction, cultural reality, and organizational maturity, so that these results can be benched against executive leadership expectations.

Level 1 Gap Analysis

1. Senior management reads this chapter.

2. Senior management completes Triangulation Theory Thermo Gap Analysis (*See Appendix A*).

3. These data are given to HR executive. This is done before level 2 because the research suggests that in many organizations what the senior leadership thinks are issues may not be consistent with what the workforce thinks. This first step will provide the benchmark for senior management to compare their points of view to the level 2 gap analysis results.

Level 2 Gap Analysis

1. HR executive facilitates a process to retrieve data from numerous data points (for example, below are 20 potential data points where information can be retrieved). This will provide the quantitative results.

2. HR executive initiaties an applied research study using job analysis strategies such as conference method, small groups, job shadowing, and one-on-one meetings to obtain important information. This will provide the qualitative results.

Examples of Quantitative Data Points

In addition to looking at attraction and retention metrics, other sources may be used to help determine the level of intelligence as to how the organization is performing. The output of this analysis would be defined gaps for improvement so executive leadership expectations will be achieved.

- Attraction data
- Retention data

- Exit interviews data

- Employee engagement survey data

- Disability management data (STD, LTD, WCB data)

- Employee behavioral data (e.g., workplace bullying, ethical behavior)

- Customer service survey data

- Employee counsel data

- Performance management data

- Recruiting validation data (e.g., how effective is the current selection of employees model for picking the right hires the first time)

- Industry benchmark data (e.g., compensation)

- Diversity and equal opportunity data

- Physical environment data (e.g., concerns around air quality, ergonomics, occupational health and safety concerns)

- Safety data

- Employee value proposition

- Corporate responsibility (e.g., compliance to corporate policies)

- Health and wellness data (average sick time, injuries in the workplace)

- Community relationship data (e.g., media and PR reports)

- Internal versus external promotions ratio data

- Average training budget per employee (e.g., in 2007 in Canada it was 1.8% of total compensation)

Triangulation Theory Thermo Gap Analysis (*See Appendix A*) provides a high level overview of the results and findings from the Triangulation

Theory analysis. This tool provides a visual overview of three elements with targeted areas for improvement.

Step 3—Implementation of Employer of Choice Strategy. The final step is to determine the strategic approach based on the results of the level 1 and level 2 Triangulation Theory thermo gap analysis gaps. The next step is to align and implement an action plan.

Part A: To avoid duplication in this process it's important to identify and align all current organizational initiatives to this action plan. Using the Triangulation Theory Strategic Plan (see appendix A) add the initiatives that have been determined relevant for improving identified core elements and are in need of attention. For example, any activities that are currently in place for influencing employee job satisfaction (motivation factors) such as work conditions (e.g., ergonomic study) would be put into the plan as actions to move an area from red or yellow to green.

Part B: Once all current initiatives have been added to the Triangulation Theory Strategic Plan, the next step is to determine what additional strategies and actions will be taken to move identified areas in need for improvement from red or yellow to green. Next, add these action plans to the Triangulation Theory Strategic Plan. For example, employers may get ideas as to what they could do to enhance a particular element and to build an action plan that could be added to the strategy by reviewing Branham's (2005) 54 summary checklist (see appendix B). In the end, there are no shortcuts and whatever the strategic plan is, all the pieces must be connected and aligned.

Part C: The Triangulation Theory strategic plan must be monitored and measured and, if need be, adjusted to ensure the organization is on the right track. The theory being, when an organization is committed to learn and grow in each of these elements and to close its defined gaps, it's on track to increase its attraction and retention. When executives hold this course and vision and commitment for results over time, an employer will achieve its desired outcome to become an employer of choice, with all the benefits and rewards that come with this result.

More than 75% of all corporate leaders now will agree that employee retention is a major issue; however only 15% have a plan (Fishman, 1998).

CHAPTER 3

Increasing Employee Retention

The cost to replace an employee who leaves is, conservatively, 30% of their annual salary. For those with skills in high demand, the cost can rise to a frightening 1.5 times the annual salary to replace them.
—The American Management Association

Superior business productivity and the resulting increased profits correlate directly to superior talent. Employee retention programs focus on the loyal, motivated, hard-working individuals who add value and help a company maintain its competitive edge, *not* underperformers or employees who do not want to be in the workplace. Companies that include systems to monitor turnover and respond to high quality workers in their strategic plan limit expenses in the short-term and reap the benefits of a workforce that will mature, improve, and innovate over the long-term.

Recent research highlights the increasingly negative impact of employee turnover on corporate profits:

- Voluntary turnover increased over the last year from 19.2% to 20.2%.

- The average public company loses half of its employees every four years, with a direct replacement cost of $10,000 to $50,000 per employee.

- The average time required to replace an employee has risen from 41 to 51 days, which significantly raises recruiting costs and lowers productivity.

- The typical American worker holds nearly nine different jobs before age 32.

- The total cost of losing a single position to turnover ranges from 30% of the yearly salary of the position for hourly employees to 150%.

- For a company with 100,000 employees at an average salary of $40,000, a 10% turnover rate costs $400 million. A turnover reduction of one-half percent would result in savings of $2 million.

- Corporations spend on average 36% of revenue on human capital expenses. Assuming an average rate of employee turnover of 25% and a cost associated with turnover equivalent to salary, the cost of turnover represents about 9% of revenue.

Employee turnover always happens. However, a company that includes a well thought out employee retention plan in its mandate increases the likelihood that good employees will stay. Doing the little things most employees want in order to feel comfortable and valuable makes economic sense because the most important corporate resource over the next 20 years will be human capital (the talent pool). This chapter examines the main reasons for both loyalty and turnover, discusses strategies for keeping high quality workers, and provides a model for an employee retention plan.

Winning Talent's Loyalty

Only 60% of the senior leaders at the companies studied by McKinsey & Co. in its year-long study that is the basis of the book, *The War for Talent*, were able to pursue most of their growth opportunities. Ed Michaels, a McKinsey director, says, "They have good ideas, they have money—they just don't have enough talented people to pursue those ideas." However, when asked, "Does your company make improving its talent pool one of its top three priorities?" in many companies, only 10% or 20% of corporate officers responded, "Yes."

The War for Talent cites four imperatives for attracting and keeping high potentials so that a company can gain a competitive advantage:

- **Talent Mindset**—The deeply held belief that senior leadership's most important role is building the talent pool.

- **Winning Employee Value Propositions**—Compelling reasons why a talented person would want to work for the company.

- **Robust Sourcing Strategy**—Aggressive and continuous talent recruitment for all levels of the organization.

- **Tactics to Build the Talent Pool**—Removal of underperformers so that talent can grow, development of untapped potential, and demonstration of appreciation for high performers.

After a company mandates that the talent pool is a priority, discovery of the reasons why people want to work for the firm drives recruiting and retention strategies. Money and promotions often rank low in the reasons for loyalty. Common considerations are listed on the table on the next page.

Methodologies used to obtain the specific data about why people want to work for a company include corporate climate surveys and focus groups. To discover why people want to leave, companies commonly analyze employee absence rates, frequency of use of employee counseling services, information from confidential exit interviews, and competitors' retention programs. Building loyalty requires determining what adjustments need to be made so that the culture "naturally makes quitting a poor choice."

Retention Strategies

Almost one-third of employees expect to leave their jobs within a year. "Loyalty leaders see people as assets rather than expenses, and they expect those assets to pay returns over a period of many years. . . They view asset defections as unacceptable, value-destroying failure, and they work constantly to eradicate them."

Reasons to Stay	Reasons to Leave
+ Feel respected and valued	− Conflict with direct manager
+ Pay is fair	− Organization not dealing with problem performers
+ Opportunities to develop and learn	− Underperformers get the same rewards as talent
+ Opportunities for advancement	− Only hear from manager when there is a concern
+ Enjoy the interprofessional relationships	− Toxic environment due to lack of trust
+ Feel fulfilled and challenged in the position	− Unwilling to adapt to change
+ Buy into the company's vision	− Dissatisfied with pay
+ Respect and enjoy working for direct manager	− No feedback or guidance
+ Stimulating and interesting workplace	− Corporate vision or direction not clear
+ Have fun doing the work	− Unmotivated and do not enjoy current position
+ Position is an important career stepping-stone	− Not clear about role and what is expected
+ Opportunity to gain core industry knowledge	− No respect for the leadership
+ Enjoy the mentoring program	− Not included in any decision-making
+ Personal contribution has clear value	− Personality conflict with a peer or manager
+ Sense of pride and ownership for the corporation	− Job demands are impacting life balance

When considering their strategic approach to retention, leaders face challenges in several areas:

- Identifying and recruiting talent.

- Cultural and environmental factors.

- The corporate image.

- Life balance.

Getting a mandate from the highest levels supports a strategic approach to retention. However, if a mandate does not exist, leaders can help build one by taking action steps at the management level, where loyalty is fostered.

Strategies for Identifying and Recruiting Talent

- *Create Position Profiles*—Define each position with a specific breakdown, not only of all the core skills and knowledge but also the behaviors, values, and attitudes that are important to the role. Comprehensive profiles ensure that business needs are met and they support the screening process.

- *Do a Retention SWOT Analysis*—Survey the company's strengths, weaknesses, obstacles, and threats from the employee's perspective. A SWOT analysis often reveals gaps and helps align perceptions.

- *Implement Recognition Programs*—Acknowledge strong performers on a regular basis. Structured programs that praise and/or reward employees who excel or are positive role models bring internal talent to the forefront and improve morale.

- *Develop Untapped Potential*—In addition to recruiting costs, bringing new knowledge workers (highly cognitively skilled workers) up to speed so they can be productive usually takes 12-18 months. Qualified internal candidates who are provided with a career path take less time to train up and are more likely to stay, making the large investment of time, energy, and money a good one.

- *Monitor the Competition*—Competitors not only compete for business share, they also compete for talent. Benchmark their turnover, their benefits and training, and levels of promotion from within. "Knowing what others are offering or doing helps companies to establish countermeasures or strategies."

Strategies to Improve the Culture and Environment

- *Take the Pulse of the Workplace*—Cultural elements that make an employee feel satisfied have a strong impact. Exit interviews, climate surveys, and focus groups provide important information to leaders about what employees value and what will satisfy the culture. "It's not so much opportunities for raises or promotion through the ranks that keep employees happy. The length of an employee's stay is determined largely by his relationship with a manager." Small acknowledgements, like saying "thank you" for a good day's work make a big difference because they signal leadership interest.

- *Eliminate Useless Bureaucracy*—To prevent duplication of effort and red tape, each level of bureaucracy needs a specific purpose that adds value to performance. When bureaucratic "smog" drains people, wastes time, creates confusion, and causes stress, many employees look for new jobs because everything is too difficult.

- *Offer Employee Counseling*—Employee counseling, either through human resources or an employee relations group, addresses problems with supervisors, fellow employees, policy, and procedure. In addition to equipping workers with the means to deal with such issues, management can track use of employee counseling to gather data on areas of frustration.

- *Remove Underperformers*—Zero percent turnover is unhealthy. Underperformers bring down both productivity and morale. In addition, moving out low performers frees up payroll currently locked in by employees with seniority.

Strategies to Support the Corporate Image

- *Keep Talent Connected*—People who have seen waves of downsizing, reorganizations, and off-shore outsourcing do not automatically see the rungs on the career ladder. Rather than remaining loyal to the company, these workers increasingly rely on themselves for stability, advancement, and opportunity. McKinsey concluded that companies that are best able to attract and retain talent over the long-term:

  ◊ Create smaller, more autonomous units.

  ◊ Offer greater wealth-creation opportunities for their best people, regardless of age or seniority, and compensate them on the basis of performance.

  ◊ Find ways to keep 30-year-olds connected to the larger organization and to give them exposure to people at the top so that they feel they are an integral part of the organization.

- *Senior Leadership Action*—The best way for a firm to get respect is to give it. Henry Ford was legendary for saying hello to everyone in the company on a first-name basis. If all senior leaders express interest in what employees say and implement solutions in a responsible manner, the entire corporation benefits.

- *Promote Teamwork and Knowledge Sharing*—If leaders are people-oriented, socially appropriate, and strong relationship builders, the corporation builds a positive image. In addition, when bullying or abuse of authority is not tolerated, team members feel comfortable sharing knowledge and asking questions. This type of synergy draws talent and keeps it.

- *Build Consistency and Trust*—Maintain Standard Operating Procedures that are up-to-date and reflect current thought. SOPs that bridge people, systems, structures, and processes allow leaders to be clear about performance expectations and consequences. This consistency builds trust and encourages employees to do their best work each day and to respect the company's leadership.

Strategies to Increase Employee Life Balance

- *Offer Value-Add Benefits*—Services and benefits above money (e.g., daycare in the building, fitness centre) support the corporation's value proposition. Many of the most admired companies in North America offer value-adds that acknowledge employees' lives are important.

- *Support Quality of Life Policies*—For example, only ask employees to put in extra time when it is really mission critical, not to meet self-inflicted deadlines. Many employees are now looking at the importance of life balance and are less willing to work 100 hours a week, regardless of the potential rewards. In addition, good life balance helps people maintain a healthy stress level; and healthy employees cost a company less money.

Developing a Retention Plan

Although companies across North America spend billions of dollars each year to stay on the cutting edge of technology, 49% of businesses have no formal strategy for retention. The results are predictable: 75% of executives surveyed by McKinsey said that their companies either don't have enough talent sometimes or that they are chronically short of talent.

Effective retention plans support the corporate succession strategy and focus on the following areas:

- **Turnover and Talent Pool Targets**—Measurable goals set by senior leadership during strategic planning.

- **Corporate Culture**—Employee satisfaction level, overall morale, and value propositions.

- **Strategic Recruiting**— Recruiting and hiring processes that assist in identifying talent.

- **Career Development**—Growth opportunities that help people realize their full potential and a competitive reward system.

When considering each of the above focus areas, getting agreement from senior leaders on the following questions assures a consistent approach:

- What kind of [turnover rate, depth of talent pool, corporate culture, recruiting effort, career development] does the organization want to provide?

- What are the organization's strengths and weaknesses in this area?

- What are the short- and long-term goals for improving in this area?

- Who will be the champion that monitors this area and reports to senior management on both improvements and declines?

- What methodology will be used to evaluate this area in regard to retention and how frequently will it be monitored?

The Employee Retention Plan Model on the next page maps the basic process for designing an employee retention plan.

Employee Retention Plan Model

❶ Determine Turnover and Talent Pool Targets

Action Steps	Questions
1. Create a team to design and review the plan. 2. Delineate the monetary costs of turnover, including all separation and replacement expenses. 3. Assess the depth of the talent pool. 4. Decide what percentage of employees are underperforming. 5. Gather data on how many employees will cycle out over the next 5 years (e.g., retire, leave due to life events such as illness, etc.) 6. Get agreement from senior leaders on a healthy level of turnover. 7. Get agreement from senior leaders on how much new talent needs to be recruited in order to meet strategic and succession goals.	• How much does the company pay per person for separation (e.g., severance pay, outplacement fees, litigation costs, exit interviews, etc.)? • How much does it cost the company to replace each level of employee (e.g., sourcing expenses, HR processing costs for screening and assessing candidates, time spent on interviews, travel and relocation, signing bonuses, orientation and training, etc.)? • What level of turnover would enable the firm to move underperformers out? • What level of turnover can be anticipated over the next 5 years? • How will the projected level of turnover impact on the succession plan? • How many high potentials are available internally?

❷ Respond to the Corporate Culture

Action Steps	Questions
1. Survey the morale and satisfaction levels of all employees. 2. Assess the corporate image, both internally and externally. 3. Determine whether the value propositions align with both the corporate strategy and the current cultural expectations. 4. Confirm that leaders' actions reinforce an atmosphere of trust. 5. Review SOPs for clarity and fairness. 6. Communicate corporate vision and values to all employees.	• Do employees generally enjoy working for the company? • Are the leaders respected both inside and outside the firm? • Do the organization's policies consider life balance needs? • Is the environment conducive to teamwork and knowledge sharing? • Do employees think that performance measures and rewards are fair? • Do all employees understand how their position contributes to the organization?

❸ Build a Recruiting Strategy

Action Steps	Questions
1. Create detailed position profiles. 2. Remove any layers of bureaucracy that do not add value. 3. Match high potentials to succession plan. 4. Assess talent gaps. 5. Compare current practices to competitors. 6. Put screening and interview standards in place. 7. Review and make necessary adjustments to on-boarding program.	• Are benefits and compensation competitive? • Does the recruiting strategy align with the corporate mandate and the succession plan? • Are there any high potentials who could be developed to fill talent gaps? • How can we determine that new hires are likely to fit into the culture? • How will we ensure that new hires are likely to stay? • How can we minimize ramp-up time?

❹ Make Career Development a Priority

Action Steps	Questions
1. Delineate which people, business, and technical skills are necessary for each position. 2. Determine what balance of classroom, experiential, and other type of training is optimal. 3. Get agreement from senior leaders on mentoring and coaching plans. 4. Define indicators of success, performance rewards, and consequences for underperformance. 5. Make step-by-step plans for each high potential.	• Is enough direct access to senior leaders included in the plan? • How are goals set and feedback given? • What milestones indicate when an individual is ready to move to the next level? • What incentives are in place for top performers? • What steps will be taken with underperformers and in what timeframe? • How are mentors and coaches chosen and trained? • Does the training offered align with business and cultural needs?

❺ Monitor the Plan	
Action Steps	**Questions**
1. Decide the best assessment tools to measure each element of the retention plan. 2. Agree on how often each element should be monitored. 3. Agree on how often the entire plan should be reviewed. 4. Determine who should be responsible for each area of the plan.	• How often should climate surveys be conducted? • Should focus groups be a regular feature of the plan? • How often should position profiles be reevaluated? • What metrics are best for assessing turnover rates? • What questions in our exit interviews will produce the most meaningful data?

In Closing

When a talented employee leaves, their knowledge and experience are lost, along with their unique skill set. A strategic retention plan that looks at the entire life cycle of employment reduces turnover and minimizes disruption of the workforce and loss of productivity. In addition to the potential cost savings of an effective employee retention strategy, companies realize such long-term benefits as:

- Increased profits because satisfied employees provide better customer service.

- Improved efficiency because motivated employees are more willing to share valuable knowledge.

- An enhanced corporate image.

- A vehicle for attracting new talent.

The time and effort required to implement an employee retention plan produces benefits that outweigh the costs many times over. Industry leaders who are concerned with developing their company's profit potential make retention not only a focus but also a priority.

CHAPTER 4

Slowing Down Turnover

Companies that manage people right will outperform companies that don't by 30% to 40%. — Jeffrey Pfeffer
The Human Equation: Building Profits by Putting People First

Employee turnover is always going to happen. The purpose of this chapter is to discuss the Employee Retention Model to increase the likelihood the right employees will stay. In other words, find out what's not meeting the productive employees' needs and work to correct it. The result: increased attraction and retention. The paradox is that many companies are still cutting positions, but at the same time are trying to keep top talent in the workforce.

My research shows what I call the big three challenges above and beyond pay and benefits for keeping employees (each represents a beneficial outcome for organizations):

- Employee feels respected and valued.

- Employee perceives they have effective leadership (direction) and management (skilled manager).

- There is a defined career plan for them for advancement within the organization.

Following are other observations of what contributes to staff turnover in many workplaces:

- Employees don't believe they have the support resources or leadership needed to do the job well.

- There's a lack of trust in the workplace. There is too much of a survival-of-the-fittest mentality bred into the culture. The result: the fear factor is high, which suppresses creativity and increases stress.

- Employees do not understand the need for change. They feel betrayed or for whatever reason want to take another path.

- Confusing reward and bonus systems that don't align performance to pay, e.g., given for favoritism, not productivity.

- Employees feel unappreciated because of a lack of meaningful feedback and information as to what they are doing.

- Cultural incongruence—the company promotes one message to the public, but behind the scenes no one believes. This environment type is so confusing that employees forget what they are there for and often lose passion for their job.

- No clear vision or defined plan for employees to follow. The vision is a crisis-to-crisis view with the emergency-of-the-day as the focus. This creates a great deal of second-guessing and wondering what employees are supposed to be doing.

- Corporate goals are not in line with employees' goals.

- Employees are unsure of their roles and what is expected of them.

- Employees perceive they have poor and ineffective leadership.

- Employees don't believe they are involved in decision making, especially if it's in their area of expertise. They see themselves as devalued in this case.

- Employees perceive relationship and personality conflicts. The reason many employees leave often has nothing to do with money; it's conflict with their direct supervisors. Most personality conflicts are rooted in poor communication.

- Employees find the job is meeting their career needs, but not life balance.

Value of Employee Retention

Employee retention is a philosophical model of what an organization can do to retain its workforce. To keep employees, companies must understand what employees like and don't like. What they don't like needs to be addressed. Organizations can never satisfy all employees, but if they have a workplace that's driven to help all team members feel good about what they do, employees will more likely want to stay. For example, staff at the SASS Institute in Raleigh, North Carolina, love to work for this employer that is committed to employee engagement. The result is employee retention is high and profits continue to soar. This company understands it takes time to build strong teams, so it is committed to creating a culture where people want to stay.

All teams go through four stages of the group adaptation process before working to their potential: (Tuckman in the 1970s):

Forming—Group is starting to deal with each other and minimal work gets done.

Storming—Group is starting to address internal conflicts and members are sorting out and negotiating to just get along. Work is still minimal.

Norming—Group members are accepting their roles and are clear of their expectations. They know what they can and need to do. Safety is high so the corporation is functioning highly. Each member of the team is much more willing to help each other.

Performing—Group members are working independently, doing their jobs to maximum potential. The team is performing at an outstanding level and has learned how to increase productivity, make decisions, share resources, and create independent satisfaction.

Often when there is high turnover of staff, the team is stuck in the first two phases. The solution is to get the team through phase three and on to the fourth phase, performing.

To help create a culture where groups and individuals can be engaged, it is of strategic value for an organization to understand the benefits of an employee retention model, such as:

- Increased ability to improve employee satisfaction.

- Increased employee satisfaction increases employee attraction and retention.

- Increased customer service and profits.

- Less conflict and stress.

- Keep the talent pool deeper. The talented are less likely to be motivated to leave just for money when the workplace meets their needs and they see a positive culture.

- Increased loyalty in employees when they know their employer is interested in their perceptions and values.

- Increased company effectiveness. When implementing employee retention programs, companies discover their employees have many valuable suggestions to increase efficiency.

- Enhanced communications in the workplace.

- Increased clarity in the workplace. A business is a living process and it's not good enough to adhere to a static set of goals; employees need to know the day-to-day changes in direction.

- Increased team building and self-leadership so more employees take responsibility for themselves and work more effectively as part of a team.

Breakdown of Employee Retention

Following is a breakdown of things to consider when developing employee retention. This section provides an overview of concerns that represent the origin of employee turnover.

Evaluate what's happening in the workplace on a consistent and regular basis to ensure that the staff is satisfied with the leadership, vision, operations, and management styles.

TIP—The following methodologies are a few examples of how to stay in touch with employees' perceptions: use the Triangulation Theory (see chapter 2), focus groups, engagement surveys, and staff meetings. A great side benefit of doing evaluations on a regular basis is that it helps senior leadership stay focused on the importance of retention. For many employees, all they need to hear is "thank you" for a good day of work. Rewards don't always mean money or benefits; many times some kind of acknowledgment is enough. The ultimate goal is for senior leaders to have their pulse on what is really happening out in the workplace; it's too often miles apart from what they think is happening.

Management goals are well defined. The goals must include the effective balance of four independent and important domains: *Operations Management, Products, Services, and Staff (People).*

TIP: Management must ensure that people are supported with effective training and tools so that they can stay current in the ever-changing workforce. Employees also need to have employers who are aware of the importance of life balance. It's not possible to separate employees from their homes. Even the young MBA "crash and burners" are becoming more aware of the importance of life balance.

Plan to create a proactive environment in which all employees know their roles, rules, expectations, accountabilities, and corporate values to facilitate a sense of ownership.

TIP: Plan and commit energy to employee satisfaction like any other priority. There needs to be high involvement of staff. The ultimate goal is to ensure all plans are well communicated, followed through on, and measured to gain employee trust.

Leadership of self is the new philosophical underpinning of management theories.

TIP: As Deming taught, for people to produce quality they must first be taught what quality is. Management must role model leadership skills, and then en courage each employee to take ownership, breeding a community of internally motivated employees who see themselves as valuable and important to the company.

Orientating staff to change is a continuous process.

TIP: In this Information Age, there is so much to learn and so much is changing that it's important to continue to train and inform staff. Change is always occurring, so it's important to have a healthy change model to help employees make the transitions that they are expected to make. Fear is real in corporate America. Employees need to be communicated to as much as possible as to what is happening in the workplace and what they can do to adjust to it and what support is in place.

Yearly performance appraisals that are of value when committed to an integrated performance management model that aligns people and business.

TIP: They need to be done with a sense of purpose and not just an exercise. They need to have new goals and must always be followed up on. The model will be more effective when supported by regular and useful out-of-cycle feedback.

Educate upper management as to what's needed to help employees be more effective in the workplace.

TIP: Management does not need to carry out all recommendations, but whether they do or not, they would be wise to evaluate the impact of their choice over the next 12-18 months. Management must be aware of the differences between corporate and individual needs. Employees are going to have individual goals that are separate from the company or their assigned teams' goals.

Environment and culture are important for employees to want to stay.

TIP: The environment needs to be safe physically and the culture will benefit when each employee perceives they are a part of a team. To do this they need to perceive there is a fair and meaningful recognition that good work is recognized and appreciated.

Relationships need to be healthy in the workplace. Broken or weak relationships create miscommunication and conflict, and influence employees to move on.

TIP: For the average employee relationships are much more important than money. In the workplace, it's common practice to put people in teams to build relationships. Team can be defined as a group working for a common purpose. Positive chemistry in a team is based on each member doing their individual job, with everyone comfortable enough to be relaxed, calm, and having fun doing what they do with high trust and communication among the group. This takes time and effort. Chemistry is important so that the group can believe in the outcome and feel comfortable to go to the boss and ask questions until the group is clear of the expected outcome. Team members support each other through the gray and frustrating times. This is why team building is so important. Managers can't assume all employees have the skills to work co-operatively and independently, which is what employers are asking for.

Evidence of knowing what is not working is not enough; it needs to be addressed. From a retention point of view, the information is good only when it's acted upon.

TIP: If management hears a certain theme over and over and doesn't act on this evidence, things will never get any better, mostly just worse. As Einstein said, "The significant problems of the world cannot be solved with the same thinking that created them." Companies need their employees to believe that they will listen to their feedback.

Trust is paramount. This is when employees believe what they are doing is being appreciated. They trust that their actions will make a difference on the long term. They know that their tasks, personal expectations, level of performance, and deadlines are important to help internal and external customers at any level. The work they do is of meaning and value and they understand "why" it is. When trust in the workplace is depleted, it takes a great deal of effort to get it back.

TIP: To have an employee be a peak performer they must trust their leaders. Leaders must answer the "Why should I trust you?" question. They can't hide from it.

Escape bureaucracy. The layers of bureaucracy are often not needed and they are usually of little value. Get rid of bureaucracy that delays responsiveness to employee needs.

TIP: Ensure that all systems have a purpose and there's not a tremendous amount of duplication and overlap. Toxic environments can develop and lead to a lack of healthy karma. When this "smog" is in the workplace, because of confusion and stress over operational bureaucracy, many employees will look for new employment.

Needs of individual employees must be addressed. Companies benefit when all employees perceive they have an impact in decision making.

Tip: Don't use Napoleon's management method. Avoid using the Napoleonic way, as he did in Waterloo, where he lost the war with poor decision making. He didn't get or accept input from others; he didn't see the entire picture, and this lost him the war. Employees need to know that they are a part of the decision making process.

Talent. Companies will benefit from acknowledging the value of their employees. Employees want to be perceived as being of value and believe the company cares. Companies must look at ways to get input from staff so they feel they have been heard.

TIP: Companies need to be creative and look at ways to keep their employees motivated and happy; this doesn't mean only money or perks. There are lots of ways to acknowledge employees. Employees feel of value as a company invests in their development as well; they believe the company is recognizing existing talent by investing in them further. An important part of any employee retention program are creative and consistent recognition programs.

Individuals need to know exactly what's expected of them. They must be aware of their daily tasks and how success is measured. It can't just be assumed; tasks need to be clearly defined.

TIP: Regardless of the level in the company, employees need to know what needs to be done daily. Whether a clerk or a CEO, there's always an expectation that needs to be obtained. All employees need to be clear on their roles and responsibilities. They know that there's work that needs to be shared, such as paperwork, phone calls, evaluating people, and filling out reports.

Organizations need to be manage information. Companies need effective knowledge transfer processes in place to ensure all processes, policies, and protocols are current and are communicated to employees.

TIP: High technology still needs people to run it. It's important that companies have strategies such as on-boarding and mentoring to ensure knowledge is shared in an organized and logical manner. This is an effective way to keep new hires and to ensure the workforce stays informed.

Never use coercion, fear, or pain as a motivator. Employees perform better when they feel safe. It's OK to have expectations and consequences for poor performance; they're predictable, like a speeding ticket.

TIP: The corporate world is competitive and with this come pressure and stress that, if allowed to control a leader can negatively influence behaviors that can be perceived as bullying, harassment, or aggression. The result can be fear. The answer to this is simple: Have a no-tolerance rule for these kinds of behaviors.

Employee Retention Model

The SUCCESS mnemonic provides organizations with a framework to build a retention strategy.

S ee the priorities and pick out the critical issues and goals that need to be addressed.

U nderstand the needs of employees from their frame of reference. Learn and practice the *Success Touch*—treating others not as you want to be treated, rather as they want to be treated, and understand that this may change, so it's important to keep asking.

C reate programs (e.g., recognition programs) and services for staff as a way to reinforce the view that they are of value and important for corporate success.

C oncentrate on what's working and reflect and learn why it is. It's important to be aware of how to help employees choose to be motivated with real, proven data points.

E valuate whether employees and upper management are working for a common goal, and if not, make the needed adjustments.

S tudy the learnings from the above steps on a regular basis to discover what else can be done to enhance the workplace and to engage the workforce.

S et the task in place that attraction and retention are core priorities and action will be taken to secure a stable and productive workforce.

In Closing

Employee retention initiatives, when well done, can take off and spread like a virus; the more it's exposed, the more it spreads, and the move it can positively infect the workplace and facilitate employee retention. The goal is to not only find what's not working but what is working and to build on it and commit to creating a place where employees would want to come and stay. There are no shortcuts to building an employee retention model; it takes commitment from senior management to make retaining a stable workforce important. One really exciting benefit of a proven retention model is positive word of mouth in the community about how good a workplace is. This can become a powerful attraction strategy because people will have evidence of how good a company is to work for.

CHAPTER 5

Developing the Pride Factor

The real voyage of discovery consists not in seeking new landscapes, but in having new eyes. —Marcel Proust

Companies today are becoming increasingly aware of the importance of attracting and retaining a stable workforce. One important focus for advancing this outcome is creating an environment that assists each employee to enhance their sense of pride in what they are doing. The term *pride factor* refers to the employee's perception of their position and sense of stake in the company. One common example is employees who have a great sense of pride in the company they work for, though lack pride for their day-to-day contribution. The big picture is too big to see where they fit. The cost of this kind of thinking is becoming increasingly clear when one looks at studies of employee retention, productivity, lost time, and the 1990s psychology stress trends.

How are the morale and productivity of your employees? If you say OK, what does this mean? Is it as good as it could be? Do you have a gut sense that something is missing that you can't quite put your finger on?

If this applies to you, then you may be frustrated as you think of all the wonderful things the company is doing for its employees (e.g., community activities, EAP, outstanding pay and benefits, and many other things you do). You may even have wondered if whatever the company does will ever be enough.

The question is, what are the consequences of this kind of thinking? It can prevent the willingness to search out the tools that may close this gap, which could be the difference between the workplace being OK and being great. It's the gap between a positive environment where employees are not happy and a place where employees are happy and much more productive.

This chapter will help you to explore some of the factors that may contribute to this perceived gap and offer several solutions as to what can be done.

Factors that Reduce the Development of Human Capital

Management Skeptics—The pride factor of leaders can sometimes be the barrier that prevents growth. People in senior management positions did not get there without having many important and helpful resources, one of them being a sense of pride in what they're doing. Leaders are taught, and seldom born. To grow, leaders need to acknowledge this fact. The first challenge is for management to accept that things can be better, and make a commitment to develop their human capital. Without the buy-in of management, none of the remaining points will ever be improved. The pride factor of leaders can sometimes be the barrier that prevents growth. It's OK for a leader to delegate and consult with people who are competent in their own area of expertise.

Solution: It makes sense for management to be skeptical in regard to developing people. The perception for some is that they don't want to stir up issues that don't need to be dealt with, but it has been proven that investing in its people is the single most effective way for a company to be effective and profitable. The solution is simple, though not easy. Leaders first need to ask themselves whether they are interested in making life better for all, and then they need to find the person who can help them set the course for this improvement. We know it works. Business books such as *The Loyalty Effect* and others have proven it. The only way for it to start in any company is for management to decide that they want to save money. The employee's development as a holistic person must be important.

Measure the Return—A manager can spend millions of dollars on a piece of equipment and measure it by what it does, but how do you measure professional development? Companies like Motorola have estimated that for every dollar they spend on professional development they obtain a $30 return. You may not be interested in formal assessments, so I offer you this. Let's assume that the average employee is working at 70% of their potential each day. This would indicate that 30% of the time they are not being as effective as they could be. Many employees have learned to pace themselves and look busy so no one will ask them to do more. Now let's look to the future and say that a Pride Program on average has helped everyone to improve their ownership, pride, and daily productivity up to 75%. How much profit does this mean to the company? If all employees were on task, did their work 5% faster, with 5% fewer errors, etc., how much would that mean for a company? The bottom line is that it's costing the company the same or even more to run at 70% vs. 75%. The truth is, the Pride Program is paid for many times over.

Solution—Once a company makes its action plan, sets out its strategies as to how to implement it (e.g., mentoring programs, train-the-trainer program, etc.) as to what it's going to do to close the gap, it's important to measure the ROI. This can be done by tracking the number of complaints and incidents, sick time, productivity, accidents, discipline issues, community feedback, customer service surveys, attitude surveys, and/or focus groups, using a pre- and post-assessment format. The purpose is two-fold: to see if the company is focusing on the right groups and to determine what needs to be improved. One final check could be the original gut check to assess how leaders sense things have improved. It's important to celebrate small change.

Understand the Natural Law of Positive Thinking—When employees don't feel that they are being heard, some will become frustrated and place the blame on the company. The majority of the workforce is motivated by external rewards; however, these alone don't guarantee happiness and productive employees. For example, if an employee is thinking negative thoughts about the company 50% of the time, how will this impact their productivity? What is this costing the company? When this gap is closed over time, from 50% to 40% to 30% and hopefully lower, what will be the return to the company?

Solution—Companies can't assume that their employees have the knowledge and skills for living life positively. Companies must offer programs for employees to develop core life skills, and not assume that they can just be positive. It will not happen. I call this kind of training Covert Professional Development, offering workshops such as wellness, parenting, relationship, smoke cessation, pain management, etc., that employees can attend voluntarily. Over time, the word will spread. This kind of strategy is pre-EAP; it's prevention and development. The goal is to help employees take ownership for their behavior and thinking.

Employees Not Feeling Valued Internally—Many employees truly don't believe their company values them. If this is true, is the company getting the most out of its employees in regard to their creativity, effort, loyalty, etc.? Three kinds of reward systems are used to motivate employees:

- Do things **FOR** them (positive rewards, e.g., company picnics, bonuses).

- Do things **AT** them (negative feedback and/or punishment with the goal of motivating employees to do their jobs).

- Do things **WITH** them. This is where leaders are out talking daily, engaging, listening, celebrating, asking for employee ideas, and working with employees to develop their competencies as professionals and people. Leaders want to be involved with employees and don't hide from them.

Solution—For an employee to feel of value they need to believe they have been heard. They don't need an employer to agree with everything they say. They need to see that they can communicate and have an impact and that their expertise is appreciated. One effective way to do this is to have every employee involved yearly in the company's succession vision planning, values, goals, and defining individual roles to increase ownership. All people in general like to be talked with, not at or told. The number one reason for conflict in the workplace is negative relationships between middle management and employees. The reason is that too many managers are managing up. When an employee believes a company is interested in them, they move from entitlement to ownership. This takes time and commitment on the company's part. The first step is to create a process that allows for open channels of communication. Mentoring programs are excellent tools to help employees learn the company values each and every one.

Not Following Through On Development Plans—Once a company becomes aware of these gaps and makes an action plan, it's important to hold the course. Too many companies fall victim of what I call the flavor of the month. Companies don't need to spend millions of dollars on canned programs to obtain desired outcomes. What they need to do is go through the due diligence of determining the need, making a plan, and following through. Regardless of the program, when you are talking about re-cultivating and reenergizing the passion and culture of a company—small or large—it can take up to three to four years for this process to take hold. People take time to move out of old belief systems. Savings achieved by decreasing loss of productivity and sick time in a large corporation are in the millions. Unfortunately, our society wants everything yesterday, but there are no shortcuts. Things will start to improve and may be adjusted or improved as the development plan is rolled out.

Solution—Make a long-term plan and have a commitment to hold the course. As a leader, you need to understand that people are the company's true power, and if you don't honor that fact the company will not be as effective as it could be. Too many companies pay for reactive realities such as sick time and lack of productivity, because they assume this is the cost of doing business. Building a culture of pride will save and generate millions of dollars.

Trust of Employees—Many employees are cautious and skeptical of change. There are three groups of employees: the Positive group that's excited the company believes in them and is going to develop the culture of the workplace; the Negative group that will not accept, believe, or want any kind of personal development, or believe things will ever change or be better; and the Elevator group, depending on who they talk to, will influence what they believe. Trust is attitude and is hard to quantify. However, when employees trust a company they will do things willingly and not believe the company is taking advantage of them.

Solution—Time, a well thought out plan, consistency, and resolve are the fuel that allows trust to be bred into the culture. By having a four-year pride development plan, a company will be on course to increase the pride of its employees. The three groups will become two (positive and negative), and over time the negatives will sort themselves out of the company or be converted. To be successful, all programs need to go through the four stages pointed out by Tuckman: forming, storming, norming, and performing. Time allows people to engage and learn.

Conclusion

Companies all over the world are looking at the question of how to balance the equation of people vs. profit. Companies like State Farm and Motorola are committed to developing people. We know a happy person is a productive person. Old school thinking like McGregor's X management styles will not work today. The rules have changed. The best way for companies to succeed and obtain the best return from their employees is to adopt self-responsibility management styles and work toward creating a learning, growing, positive, and exciting work environment that motivates to build pride in employees and profits for all. There is no better investment than seeking to understand employees' personal development needs and then providing this service.

CHAPTER 6

The Cost of Fear

The economic loss from fear is appalling. It is necessary for better quality and productivity that people feel secure. —Dr. W. Edwards Deming

Like a schoolyard bully, some managers use fear, intimidation, and aggressive behavior to gain control of their staff and colleagues. An aggressive management style is still prevalent in the corporate world, despite the well-established fact that fear has a corrosive effect on personal and organizational performance. Behavioral scientists have demonstrated that fear can contribute to the loss of honest communication, increase conflict and stress, fuel suspicion of management, and create stubborn adherence to the status quo. Resentment and hostility towards managers and the corporation further complicate the situation. Very rapidly, the work culture spins out of control as one manager uses fear to motivate their team. Team members, in turn, respond either by withdrawing or by becoming hostile themselves, which creates a new cycle of fear.

This chapter discusses fear in the workplace: how it impacts productivity, undermines authority, and severely limits a company's ability to grow. It also provides a set of strategies to decrease fear in the work culture. Ultimately, managers are responsible for the culture they create; a successful manager, however, can undo the effects of fear and transform the workplace atmosphere.

Fear Has Tangible Effects

Dr. W. Edwards Deming, an expert in organizations, wrote a great deal about the work culture and how it affects productivity and quality. In *The New Economics* he wrote, "He [the manager] needs to understand that the performance of anyone is governed largely by the system that he works in, [which is] the responsibility of management." Demings' study of organizational systems led him to focus on the psychology of the workplace. In his book, *Out of the Crisis*, he argued that negative psychological forces such as fear actually impeded progress and lowered productivity.

Following are examples from Deming of how fear enters a system and undermines its ability to function:

- An inspector, mindful of the company's target of 10% for defective product, passes borderline work to ensure the reject rate remains below 10%, out of fear of causing the loss of jobs.

- A teacher, aware of the academic standing of her students, may pass a student who is just barely below the requirements for a passing grade. The teacher's fear of harming a student's ranking will, in fact, promote the student into work they are not prepared to handle.

- A committee appointed by a manager to report on a specific issue may over-emphasize data that support the manager's contentions and dismiss data that seem to contradict the manager's view.

In other words, when fear is embedded within the work structure, fear-driven behavior becomes institutionalized. Deming insists that collective fear, in a fear driven workplace, will have a profound impact on an institution's competitiveness, productivity, and quality.

Negative Consequences of Fear

- People learn not to question directions for fear of being attacked.

- People don't feel safe to ask for clarification for fear of looking stupid.

- Managers who use fear develop an administrative-focused approach (e.g., bossing—only speak to give orders) vs. leadership-focused (e.g., coaching—looks for opportunities to teach).

- Fear of hostility creates anxiety, teaching staff to avoid interaction with management rather than seek out management for direction and growth opportunity.

- Fear of taking risks reduces creativity. Workers find it safer to do exactly as instructed and avoid scrutiny from management. As a result, fear conditions employees to lower their standards and expectations towards their own work.

- Fear creates rigid structures and makes organizations less dynamic. When the workplace becomes overly focused on dodging blame and defending decisions, the atmosphere becomes overly political. Energy is spent building alliances and developing back-up documentation. In such a culture, innovation grinds to a halt.

- Fear promotes social conformity, as standing apart from the crowd is perceived as dangerous behavior. Social conformity can lead to group think, as good people fear becoming a whistleblower and may even feel compelled to go along with unethical behavior.

- Fear prevents people from thinking and speaking up, in two ways.
  - ◊ They fear that speaking out and being wrong will lead to ridicule; this makes workers hesitant to speak.
  - ◊ They fear that being right will result in a change that will hurt them or their colleagues; this makes workers cling to the status quo. The status quo may be painful, but for many it's better than the possibility of things getting worse.

- Fear has many hidden costs; it contributes to stress, depression, and anxiety, which are associated with addictions, heart disease, cancer, and other stress related illnesses. A fear-based culture drives up sick days, lowers retention, and blocks innovation. All of these factors have real dollar costs associated with them. What is the real cost of production when the cost of fear is factored in?

- Fear blocks important information flow to senior management. Because each rung of the reporting structure is focused on defending choices and avoiding responsibility, information is filtered at each stage. Thus, much of the information that senior managers receive may be dangerously inaccurate.

- Fear focuses efforts on internal rivalry rather than external competition. When survival is the main objective, group heads may feel justified making decisions that negatively impact another group or team. When success is the objective, groups pay more attention to each other and how their choices will help position the firm in the marketplace.

Actions for Driving Fear Out of a Culture

Once fear is entrenched in a culture, removing it is difficult. It can only be replaced with a sense of security, self-respect, and personal value. Managers can take action to make their staff feel safe, first by taking responsibility for their own behavior, and second by refusing to accept hostility from others.

Management Strategies for Driving out Fear

- Be willing to listen to what employees are saying.

- Be approachable (everyone gets treated with respect, regardless of title) and never abuse authority.

- Follow up on what you say, and be consistent so employees can learn to trust your word. Promote the model, "I do what I say."

- Don't allow bullies to operate in our organization.

- Promote leadership by influencing and positive role modeling.

- Acknowledge that it is the employees, those who do the day-to-day work, who are the real knowledge and functional experts.

- Create an open community where information and decisions are shared and where questions are welcome.

- Demonstrate that risk and failure are a part of the learning process.

- Don't inhibit people from thinking creatively or for wanting to solve their own problems.

- Be willing to give people more than one chance to succeed.

Conclusion

As Deming taught, the corporate world must understand that aggressive management is an inefficient motivator and costs corporations millions in decreased employee engagement and increased turnover. Aggression creates fear, and fear creates a culture where good work is almost impossible to accomplish. Fear inhibits organizational effectiveness by conditioning some employees to be afraid to ask for direction or make suggestions. Corporations need to realize that performance comes from people, not products or assets. A workforce that is empowered, one that feels valued and secure, is more likely to devote its energy to performance. Every leader's role is to ask themselves what they, personally, are doing to remove fear from their corporate culture.

CHAPTER 7

What Managers Need to Know

Leaders need to be willing to start with a question. What needs to be done?
— Peter Drucker

Managers Face More Complex Human Interaction

One of the most obvious ways the look and feel of business has changed over the last 20 years is the flattening of organizational structure that resulted in the removal of several layers of management.

Many organizations have become more reliant on outsourcing services, project management, and sharing of resources, resulting in increased cross-team dependency.

Flattened organizations were created to reduce waste and redundancy and to empower more people in the day-to-day decision-making process. As a direct consequence of this strategy, managers in these flattened organizations face an increased complexity in human interaction.

People have to want to do what a manager needs them to do, in contrast to the old command-and-control management models in which employees complied out of fear. To be successful today, managers must navigate not only their reports but, in many cases, their peers and vendors to achieve their targets.

Key decision-makers can no longer rely just on the old hierarchy command-and-control strategies, such as do it or you're fired. Managers must have a new set of skills that promotes relationship-building and collaboration.

Some managers are locked into the command-and-control model, and each day they become more frustrated, angry, and isolated; they break a few more relationships until they become totally ineffective. At that point, the organization's senior leadership must determine if they want effective or ineffective managers and the consequences of both choices.

As a result, today's managers will be more successful in flattened organizations by developing their influencing skills. Influencing can be defined as the art of getting people to do things willingly without having any power over them.

There's another change worth noting that further promotes the need for influencing skills. Society as a whole has removed much of the old perceived power and authority of managers, as employee rights increased to diminish psychological abuse and harassment.

As a result, managers have much less deference than they once did. A manager who is outstanding at influencing skills is better able to influence their employees to work for them, not because they have to, but because they want to.

Dale Carnegie, author of *How to Win Friends and Influence People,* promoted a simple idea: Influencing is directly linked to trust. To build trust, it's paramount to first gain rapport, which is the foundation of trust.

For more than 70 years, Carnegie's simple truth has helped companies around the world learn how to better interact and socialize as a team without fear. Managers who can take this basic concept of treating employees and peers as if they were their best customer will eventually build strong bridges and more trust. These managers will get more results.

As a business coach, one of the biggest crises I see in the workforce is management ineffectiveness. Getting the title of manager is nothing more than an opportunity; it's not a privilege or a right.

There are no shortcuts to influencing people; it takes a great deal of effort, time, and energy. However, this investment nets better relationships, increased employee trust and commitment, a collaborative and supportive work environment, and employee loyalty and retention.

Many people do not leave jobs; they quit their managers. Managers who do not develop strong emotional intelligence, social intelligence, communication skills, and interpersonal skills struggle to influence people to want to work collaboratively for and with them.

Being an effective manager in today's world requires more tools than industry smarts. It requires people-smarts and a commitment to not just give lip service. There are too many out there who claim to be collaborative but still operate like they're in the old command-and-control hierarchies.

Beware of Group Thinking

Over the years, I have been active in developing teams, from coaching university football and building corporate teams with senior leaders through executive coaching, to delivery of professional development programs designed to facilitate team-building.

I have seen teams fail for many reasons. I have also seen managers perplexed as to why talented professionals can't perform to their potential and leaders get caught up in power struggles with teams.

Social psychologist Irving Janis observed a phenomenon in teams that led to their under-performing. He called this concept group think. Group think occurs when a team becomes so enmeshed it loses objectivity to the point that it rationalizes its behaviours that result in ineffective decisions and under-performance.

Some of the risks of group think are:

- Members become over-confident in the group's ability.

- The group doesn't use practical judgment and takes unnecessary risks.

- Members almost stop thinking and trust the group's decisions without challenging them.

- The team judges the outside world to the point that outsiders are viewed almost as the enemy.

- The group creates an atmosphere where it is not perceived safe for members to express opinions against the group think.

- The group presents that all decisions have been made unanimously.

- Group members become protective of each other, leaving the manager feeling like an outsider.

The warning signs of group think can vary and include:

- The manager feels the team is not motivated or committed to quality results.

- The team does not respond positively to feedback from the manager.

- The manager feels pushed and there's tension and over-rationalization within the group.

- The manager feels almost like an outsider.

- Team members are not performing to their potential, based on past performance.

- Managers are becoming frustrated to the point of feeling they are in a constant power struggle or conflict with the team.

Strategies for Eliminating Group Think

- Ensure the team has clearly defined roles and expectations; establish how each member will be evaluated on productivity.

- Ensure the team is clearly trained on how decisions are made and evaluated within the organization.

- Ask questions in regard to preferences for getting tasks done and how members will evaluate and measure quality and productivity, based on defined roles and expectations.

- Give each member an opportunity to be the group's quality control member, whose role is to be the critical eye and to ensure that all group work is presented to management at the expected standards.

- Bring in outside experts who have a proven track record, to challenge group think on a topic to reduce group nepotism.

- Assign each team member a mentor and provide an opportunity to share critical learning with each other, to increase the opportunity for dialogue on diverse perspectives and views.

- Ask each member of a group to take the role of critic and ask members what they think the group is doing well and what it could do differently or benefit from learning.

- Don't personalize group think and feel you have been isolated. A leader's job is to decide whether group think is blinding the group's potential and organizational results.

- Help the team discover what group think is, to promote the importance of diverse perspective and individual strategic, creative, and critical thinking.

Good Intentions Are Not Enough

Have you ever had someone define an expectation and later found out what they said would happen didn't?

How did you feel about the leader after that incident?

I had a leader once say, after the fact, "You know, I really expected this training to happen for you, but once I started into it, I learned I couldn't make it happen. So it is the way it is."

As I reflected on that, I thought to myself, perhaps this is true. However, the leader promised it would not be an issue and didn't communicate any red flags or concern as to why I might not be able to attend the training.

Now I wondered if this person ever did anything or was ever aware of the number of times they sent out false expectations. I wonder if the leader ever got it that within a short time, he or she lost credibility with me. Even worse, I didn't trust or respect this person as my leader.

This reminds me of a sound piece of leadership advice: under-promise and over-deliver on what you say you can do. Also, keep in mind that good intentions alone are not enough to motivate and build trust in a workforce.

This is a simple coaching tip with powerful implications for a leader's credibility and capacity to motivate and influence people to follow them.

As a business coach, I have witnessed first-hand how leaders can quickly lose credibility with their teams by making decrees and calls to action and then not following through or making them happen.

There are many variables at play for any business leader, such as politics, the economy, and business culture. One variable you don't want to face is loss of your peers' or employees' trust in your word.

For the most part, people in the workplace keep score through an evidence-based orientation, meaning all expectations are defined and set and are objectively measured.

For example, many companies post on their walls value statements that frame the expectations for the kind of workplace the organization is committed to. However, when managers fail to model the values by their behaviours, the intentions and purpose of the decree are lost.

This is a macro example but can be related to any leader. What leaders say they will do sets the expectations that people will objectively measure them by. Falling short of these expectations will take away credibility and trust.

Dos and Don'ts for Framing Expectations

- Do follow up on expectation timelines to ensure results have been obtained.

- Do keep in mind how important it is to help employees meet their needs in the workplace.

- Do accept expectations that have been discussed are important and will influence employees' views of your credibility.

- Do actively and openly discuss with employees any risks and challenges for meeting an expectation.

- Do engage employees in discussions when looking for solutions to achieve an outcome.

- Do write down and track your commitments (e.g., time frame, parties, and expectations).

- Don't make absolute promises when there are other forces involved (e.g., other decision-makers).

- Don't avoid employees when you know an event or situation is not going to happen; share your information.

- Don't make agreements without knowing all the facts.

- Don't make decisions and determine an action without knowing all the facts.

- Don't assume your employees know what you mean when framing an expectation. Simply ask: "OK, let's check to ensure we are all on the same page. What expectations are you hearing?"

- Don't make excuses. When you make a mistake, own it.

Leadership and Judgment

Each day a business leader enters the workplace they are required to make decisions. And whether their decisions are good or ineffective influences how colleagues rate their business judgment capacity.

Leaders grow by making mistakes and, in fact, great leaders teach others to fail fast and learn from their mistakes fast. However, the wrong kinds of mistakes, regardless of where a leader is in their development, can be career ending.

The business judgment model outlined below will assist leaders to make good decisions on mini, medium and major issues.

All business judgment is influenced by a leader's capacity to consider variables such as risk, opportunity, influences, drivers, and urgency. The combination of these affects the leader's judgment to take action and the direction and expectation of the action.

A leader's ultimate success in business often comes down to their ability to think strategically and critically and to be decisive and clear when they make a final decision.

The model outlined below is straightforward. It describes an element to be considered and then lists questions to facilitate making a decision. When faced with making a decision, run it through each of the four elements.

Once you complete the process you will have done strategic business decision due diligence. Keep in mind that as a leader you always will be held accountable for your final decision, so it's worth discovering a model to assist you in making sound decisions. The more you practice a model like this, the more you will stay strategic and make decisions based on facts, not emotion.

Business Judgment Model

Fear—Human beings got to the top of the food chain because they understood the power of fear. In the business world, fear can influence emotions, so to be an effective leader you need to be able to manage emotion and not allow it to manage you.

Questions: Why does this decision have to be made? If you make a mistake, what are the risks, and how do you know? What support systems can you use to ensure you are separating facts from emotion?

Facts—Thinking and knowing are two different things. Making the right decisions requires having correct information. Remove assumptions and be willing to take the time to get your facts right.

Questions: What process are you going to use to get the facts? What are the facts? How can you be sure you have them right?

Future—A leader's business judgment impacts their future and that of others. Be mindful of the consequences of a decision to all people directly and indirectly impacted by it.

Questions: Knowing the facts, what is the best decision? Why is this the best decision? Test the decision: Would you want to see it on the front page of tomorrow's newspaper? If not, why?

Fulcrum—The time constraints and urgency of a decision influence when it has to be made. Know what levers are moving the decision along so you are aware of the best time to take action. Timing a decision correctly can be the difference between its being accepted or rejected.

Questions: What's the right time for the decision (immediate, wait for an event to happen, etc.)? Not taking action is a decision: What time and date are you committed to take action? What's the cost of doing nothing?

Performance Results Must Be Aligned With Business

As a business coach, my roots are in behavioural science and I often use this background to help clients examine options and opportunities to manage their organization more effectively.

One strategy with some executive leaders is to look at the organization as a whole and explore the relationship of individual performance behaviours to organizational performance results.

The logic for this approach is that demonstrative effective or ineffective behaviours jump out. However, changes in an organization, whether effective or ineffective, are often not understood or it's not obvious how they directly impact overall performance.

Every organization experiences some kind of change all the time and the consequences of changes in behaviour (simple or complex) can have a global impact on the organization. Stimulus response psychology teaches that people can become conditioned in the workforce, based on the responses provided from their environment.

Both positive and negative stimuli can impact behaviour. This creates conditioning and learning as to how things are and will be.

Assumptions about how things are or limiting beliefs, when put under a microscope and opened for examination, can facilitate a process for leaders to look at new opportunities and options to add new behaviours and remove old ones.

The 3-D approach outlined below is a way for leaders to do a critical behavioural path review of their organization or team. Professionals trained in behavioural science can be helpful in facilitating such a process.

Whether an organization is an operation with 100 people or 100,000, the below logic has utility when supported by key decision-makers. The only change is scale and approach; the fundamentals are the same. This process helps ensure all the parts are connected to their full potential.

Discovery

What is the critical behavioural path for success? All business operational processes have a clear beginning, middle, and end. Reviewing the individual performance behaviours in each of these processes is an important review and educational step.

What is the reality of how day-to-day performance is achieved? Even with well-defined policies and procedures, operational flow charts and work standards with the best intentions, sometimes things are not the way they were designed. This process is a simple functional gap analysis.

What options and opportunities are there? Answers to questions, such as "We have always done it this way" or "just because," can be a potential sign for new opportunities and options. The goal is to challenge assumptions and to look for new opportunities to add or remove behaviours from the critical behavioural path.

Decisions

The first step is deciding what opportunities and options have been discovered and make sense to think about and consider.

Examine how the new options and opportunities will create organizational change and determine the risks and rewards, as well as the timing.

To achieve change, organizations need to build in a process that provides new conditioning and learning until the change becomes automatic and ingrained. Before considering making change, senior management must be on board and committed.

Direction

Before implementing the new direction, the behavioural critical path (e.g., job function changes, quality control checks, metrics, feedback systems) needs to be reviewed to ensure the path is complete, and if followed to the standards and expectations, the organizational performance results will be improved.

Rolling out a new critical path may require communication strategy, training and a tracking system.

Implement the new options and opportunities. Repeating this process each mid-year can be a precursor for strategic planning and business planning.

Managers Need An Annual Tune-up

How effective were you as a manager last year?

Every person who manages people will benefit from doing a detailed self-evaluation of his or her progress in the previous year. The action plan below will help you evaluate what you did well and what you want to do this year.

Read the description of each of the 20 management activities and say whether you achieved the outcome or met your or others' expectations. After completing the survey, determine what two activities are your biggest strengths.

It's important to be aware and continue developing your strengths. If you fell short of your expectations, pick the top two areas that you believe doing nothing about in the near- and mid-term could negatively affect your future growth potential.

Once you have your top two developmental activities, put an action plan in place to reach your goals by the end of this year.

The action plan should address these issues:

- I was a positive role model; I led by example.

- I was prepared, anticipated needs, was on time, ready, and organized 90%+ of the time.

- I developed a clear strategic plan that drove my business plan design. I clearly broke out the individual goals and milestones needed to achieve the business plan.

- I followed up on a regular basis with all goals, assignments, delegations and commitments 90%+ of the time.

- I demonstrated my commitment to this by actively engaging staff and peers in regular interactions that were engaging and stimulating.

- I trusted my staff by allowing them to make decisions and be responsible for functions where my direct involvement was not mandatory.

- I helped each person on my team focus on their strengths and did not try to enforce a team model.

- I facilitated my personal development and my team members' development with interest and excitement.

- I achieved 90% of my defined business and performance objectives.

- I demonstrated the ability to align my workforce with all processes in a productive and efficient way.

- I had open and honest two-way communications.

- I used daily, weekly, and monthly set metrics and measures to ensure we were on track to achieve our goals, to set priorities, and to make decisions.

- I was committed to continuous improvement and looked for strategies to increase efficiency and save costs, time, and resources.

- I had a proven effective meeting format to maximize the use of meeting time.

- I understood how critical performance management is for developing and retaining our workforce.

- I consciously developed a set of strategies and practices to retain employees.

- I worked with my team to set priorities in a collaborative environment to ensure everyone was clear on priorities and the rationale for these decisions.

- I was committed to providing outstanding customer service.

- I came to work each day excited to work.

- As I look back at the last year, I am pleased with my contribution to the organization and feel my role is of value.

Organizational Intelligence

The first intelligence studied was cognitive intelligence. Next came emotional intelligence research that reported that IQ represents only 20% of the equation for predicting a person's potential; the other 80% is based on emotional intelligence.

Daniel Goleman, author of the landmark book *Emotional Intelligence,* then moved on to author another book on the role of social intelligence. Educator Howard Gardner's seminal work around multiple intelligences impacted the way educators evaluated a learner's capacity to learn. Interestingly, all of the above intelligences have one common element: they identify behaviours and skills for predicting future capacity and success.

This section introduces another intelligence that will help predict how effectively people will work together to assist an organization to achieve its full potential. I call this organizational intelligence. Social psychology teaches that social interactions influence how people think and feel. Thus the perception of how people think and feel about an organization impacts how they behave and how that impacts organizational success.

How much organizational intelligence a company has depends on how effective its leaders are at influencing and facilitating the 15 core elements listed below. These will ultimately define the organization's level of organizational intelligence.

- **Culture**—what people really believe to be true about the organization.

- **Commitment**—the accepted work ethic and level of commitment demonstrated.

- **Co-operation**—how people work together as teams to achieve agreed-upon organizational goals.

- **Caring**—how people support and protect each other's interests, as well as the organization's.

- **Consistency**—the level of commitment and pride to do quality work.

- **Career path**—the level of job satisfaction and career opportunities perceived.

- **Controls**—the degree of integrity to follow processes, protocols, standards, ethics, and laws.

- **Compensation**—how satisfied and competitive people think their pay and benefits are.

- **Congratulations**—how people perceive they are acknowledged and recognized.

- **Change**—how flexible people are to new ways and ideas for doing business.

- **Conflict**—how effective people are at resolving conflict and solving problems collaboratively.

- **Captain**—how positive and trusting people are in their leadership.

- **Communication**—how effective people are at communicating both orally and written.

- **Carrying through**—how convinced people believe leadership does what it says.

- **Customer service**—how effective the organization is at providing excellent customer service, both internally and externally.

One metaphor to help leaders have a frame of reference as to how to manage the 15 core elements of organizational intelligence is to think of a stereo equalizer and each core element is a button that has its own setting.

Three simple steps to facilitate the development of organizational intelligence: 1) Objectively assess and evaluate each core element; 2) If necessary, make a plan and take action to improve core elements that need attention; 3) Regularly monitor, measure, and adjust each core element. Only through a continuous process will an organization develop its organizational intelligence to its fullest potential.

In the end, development of organizational intelligence requires senior leaders who are committed to the above process of facilitating and growing it. A company will achieve its fullest potential only when the entire workforce is heading in the same direction in regard to thinking and feeling, as these directly influence employee daily behaviours that synergistically define the organization's ultimate success or failure.

Workforce Planning

Does your business need quality employees to be successful?

Though this may sound like a rhetorical question, it's not meant to be. It's meant to be a strategic question that will provide the framework for this section. Organizations need quality employees to be successful and to have them they need to be outstanding at workforce planning, implementation, and stabilization.

Workforce planning is a flexible process that adapts to business needs. It's similar to a supply chain in a factory where many drivers influence cost and quality of the final product.

Perhaps the first workforce planning question should be, "What functions will people perform and why?" From this question job descriptions, workforce numbers, compensation, and management structures are determined.

Workforce planning must then move from just being an accounting activity to an organizational design and learning reality, to align the people factor to business needs.

Five core points that influence workforce planning success:

Attracting a Workforce—Companies are experiencing a workforce shortage. Demographic research suggests over the next five years they will be short millions of workers. The psychology of why employees come and go is mission critical for executive leaders. If I were on a board of directors today, I would have two questions for the CEO: "Why would an employee want to work and stay with our organization? Where are your facts?" Understanding the employee value proposition is important for attracting a workforce.

Quality of Employee—For an organization to understand what quality employees would look like there must be clear definitions (e.g., defined core competencies, experiences, training and traits). Organizations can't assume; they need to do research and due diligence to get the right facts. This ensures workforce planning includes facts for implementing a fair and defendable selection process, succession planning, knowledge transfer, capacity mapping and promotion process.

Employee Engagement—Having a workforce that's not engaged may in some cases be no better than having no workforce. When employees don't see or link how their assigned tasks impact an organization's success, don't believe they are doing meaningful work, see no job or career mobility or don't trust management, workforce disengagement results.

Employee Retention—Turnover costs are staggering. Turnover can't be eliminated, but it can be slowed down. Retention is not just keeping employees, it's also keeping quality ones. Every company has a pool of stars that are its A team. But just as important is the B team. These employees are competent in their roles, are great at following, are loyal, want to do a job, and do the majority of the work. This group needs to be recognized and acknowledged on a regular basis. They don't expect huge bonuses; however, they expect to be rewarded for good work. A paycheque is just not good enough today. Genuine appreciation, tokens of thanks and deserved perks go a long way.

Executive Reaction—This is actions senior management takes to address the above four points. Too many senior managers' views of what's important to a workforce are not the same as the workforce's. My advice for senior management is if you want the truth unfiltered, use external resources that can get you the facts without emotion or agenda. This will help stabilize the workforce planning process and allow you to continue to search for ways to influence the workforce's head, heart, and hands.

Workforce planning is not a static process; it's dynamic and takes continued commitment to quality. Gone are the days of employers having a large flock to pick from. Today's flock is smart; they know what they want; they know their rights; and they have clear expectations. Employers who work with employees to help them meet their expectations will have a workforce committed to meeting company expectations.

REFERENCES

Amble, B. (2005). *Employee disengagement a global epidemic.* Retrieved April 22, 2008, from www.management-issues.com/2006/8/24/research/employee-disengagement-a-global-epidemic.asp

Ambler, T. & Barrow, S. (1996). The employer brand. *Journal of Brand Management, Vol. 4,* 185-206.

APA Monitor (January, 2008). *APA's stress in America survey.* Washington: APA.

Bennis, W. (1990a). *Why leaders can't lead.* San Francisco: Jossey-Bass.

Bernthal, P. R. & Wellins, R. S. (2005). *Retaining talent: A Benchmarking study.* Retrieved November 10, 2005, from http://www.ddiworld.com

Beverly, K. & Jordan-Evan, S. (2005). *Love'em or lose'em. Getting good people to stay.* San Francisco: Berrett-Koehler Publisher.

Blanchard, K. & Bowles, S. (1998). *Gung ho!: Turn on the people in any organization.* New York: Marrow.

Bontis, N. (2001). *Intellectual capital ROI: A casual map of human capital antecedents and consequences.* Retrieved May 20, 2008, from http://www.business.mcmaster.ca/mktg/nbontis//ic/publications/JICBontisFitz-enz.pdf

Branham, L. (2001). *Keeping the people who keep you in business.* New York: American Management Association.

Branham, L. (2005). *The 7 hidden reasons employees leave.* New York: American Management Association.

Capon, N. (2001). *Key account management and planning.* New York: Free Press Key.

Cappelli, P. & Hermina, I. (2001). Finding and keeping the best people. *Harvard Business Review.* Boston: Harvard Business School Press.

Cascio, W. F. (2003). *Managing human resources: Productivity, quality of life, profits* (6th Ed.). New York: McGraw-Hill.

Catlette, B. (2000). *Contented cows give better milk.* New York: Contented Cow Partners.

Clark, K. (1999). Why it pays to quit. *US News and World Report, Annual Career Guide 2000.*

Collins, J. (2001). *Good to great: Why some companies make the leap... and others don't.* New York: Collins.

Cooperrider, D. L. & Srivastva, S. (1987). Appreciative inquiry in organizational life. In R. Woodman & W. Pasmore (eds.). *Research in Organizational Change and Development: Volume 1* (129-169). Greenwich, CT: JAI Press.

Deloitte Consulting LLP and CFO Research Services. (November 2005). *IQ matters: Senior finance and IT executives seek to boost information quality.* CFO Publishing Corp.: Boston.

Deming, W. E. (1994). *The new economics.* Cambridge, MA: MIT Press. Quoted from The W. Edwards Deming Institute website: http://www.deming.org/theman/teachings.html. Retrieved August 19, 2005.

Deming, W. E. (2000). *Out of the crisis.* Cambridge, MA: MIT Press.

Dobbs, K. (2001). Knowing how to keep your best and brightest. *Workforce.*

Fieldglass consulting. (2008). *Breaking down the barriers: A holistic approach to acquiring human capital research results.* Chicago, IL.

Fishman, C. (1998). The war for talent. *Fast Company, 16.*

Gladwell, M. (2002). *The tipping point: How little things can make a big difference.* New York: Back Bay.

Glasser, W. (1998. *Choice theory. A new psychology of personal freedom.* New York: HarperCollins.

Glebbeck, A. C. & Bax, E. H. (2004). Is high employee turnover really harmful? An empirical test using company records. *Academy of Management Journal, 47*(2), 277-286.

Graham, M. W. & Messner, P. E. (1998). Principals and job satisfaction. *International Journal of Educational Management,* 12:5, 196.

Griffeth, R. W., & Hom, P. W. 1988. A comparison of different conceptualizations of perceived alternatives in turnover research. *Journal of Organizational Behavior, 9*: 103-111.

Harris, J. & Brannick, J. (1999). *Finding & keeping great employees.* New York: American Management Association.

Herzberg, F. (1968). One more time: How do you motivate employees? *Harvard Business Review 46*(1), pp 53-62.

Herzberg, F. (1982). *The managerial choice: To be efficient and to be human.* Salt Lake City, UT: Olympus Publishing.

Herzberg, F., Mausner, B., & Snyderman, B. B. (1959). *The motivation to work.* New York: John Wiley.

IMB Global Business Solutions. (2008). *IMB global human capital study.* New York.

In search of the ideal manager. (2003). Retrieved May 16, 2006, from http/ www.cubiks.com

Jones, E. E. & Harris, V. A. (1967). The attribution of attitudes. *Journal of Experimental Social Psychology 3,* 1-24.

Kaye, B. & Jordan-Evans, S. (2002). *Love 'em or lose 'em: Getting good people to Stay.* New York: Berrett-Koehler Publishers.

Kazanjian, K. (2007). *Exceeding customer expectations.* New York: Random House.

Kepner-Tregoe (1999-December). Turnover calculating its true impact. *Success in Recruiting and Retaining Newsletter,* National Institute of Business Management.

Larson, M. (2006). Restive workforce less satisfied but not yet ready to change jobs. *Workforce Magazine.*

Lermusiaux, Y. (2005). *Calculating the high cost of employee turnover.* Retrieved October 30, 2005, from http://www.ilogos.com/en/ expert-views/articles/strategic/20031007_YL.html.

Mayo, E. (1945). *The social problems of an industrial civilization.* New Hampshire: Ayer.

Manpower. (2007). *Talent shortage study: 2007 global results.* http://files.shareholder.com/downloads/MAN/164219164x0x87523/a49c96c9-cbfe-47ac-9207476be0e84c20/Talent%20Shortage%20Survey%20Results_2007_FINAL.pdf

McClelland, D. C. (1988). *Human motivation.* Boston: Cambridge University.

McKinsey & Company (2001). *The war for talent: Organization and leadership practice.* New York: McKinsey & Company.

Michaels, E., Handfield-Jones, H., & Axelrod, B. (2001). *The war for talent.* Boston: Harvard Business School Press.

Minchington, B. (2005). *Employee branding definition.* Retrieved April 7, 2008, from www.Shrm.org

Mossholder, K. W., Settoon, R. P., & Henagan, S. C. (2005). A relational perspective on turnover examining structural, attitudinal, and behavioral predictors. *Academy of Management Journal, 48*: 607-618.

Nebraska Department of Economic Development. (2001). *Building the foundations of workforce development: A business and community guidebook.* Lincoln, NE.

Nicholson, N., & West, M. (1989). Managerial job change: Men and women in transition. *The Academy of Management Review, 14*, 4, 604-606.

Nonaka, I. & Takeuchi, H. (1995). *The knowledge-creating company.* New York: Oxford University Press.

Putzier, J. (2001). *Get weird! 101 innovative ways to make your company a great place to work.* New York: ANACOM.

Reichheld, F. (1996). *The loyalty effect: The hidden force behind growth, profits, and lasting value.* Cambridge, MA: Harvard Business School Press.

Reichheld, F. F. (2001). *The loyalty effect: The hidden force behind growth, profits, and lasting value.* Boston: Harvard Business School Press.

Saratoga Institute (1995). *Study of the emerging workforce.* Los Angeles: Interim Services.

Saratoga Institute. (1997). *Retention management: A report on strategies, practices, and trends.* New York: American Management Association.

Schneider, F., Gruman, J., & Coutts, L. (Eds.). (2005). *Applied social psychology.* London, UK: Sage Publications.

Scott, B. (2005). *Top grading.* New York: Penguin.

Senge, P. M. (1990). *The fifth discipline: The art & practice of the learning organization.* New York: Doubleday.

Slater, R. (1999). *Jack Welch and the GE way.* New York: McGraw Hill.

Smye, M. & Wright, L. (1996). *Corporate abuse how lean and mean.* New York: Macmillan.

Stafford, D. (1999, March 9). A hero in hiring. *Kansas City Star.*

Taleo Research (2007). *Talent management in a down economy white paper.* Dublin, CA.

The Conference Board (2007). *U.S. job satisfaction declines.* Retrieved March 12, 2008, from http://www.conference board.org/utilities/pressDetail.cfm?press_ID=3075

Tietjen, M. & Myers, R. (1998). Motivation and job satisfaction. *Management Decision, 36* (4), 226.

Tracy, B. (2000). *The 100 absolutely unbreakable laws of business success.* San Francisco: Berret-Koehler.

U.S. Department of Labor. (2004). *Bureau of Labor Statistics. Job openings and labor turnover survey.* Retrieved October 30, 2005, from http://www.dol.gov/

Wall, T. D. & Stephenson, G. W. (1970). Herzberg's two-factor theory of job attitudes: A critical evaluation and some fresh evidence. *Industrial Relations Journal, 1* (3), 41-65.

Walton, M. (1986). *The Deming management method.* New York: Perigee.

Western Compensation & Benefits Consultants (2007). *Employee attraction and retention e-pulse survey.* Retrieved from April 10, 2008, from http://www.wcbc.ca/news

APPENDIX A

Triangulation Theory Thermo Gap Analysis

Corporation: _____

Date: _____

For each of the following verticals, use the results of the employer of choice analysis and assessment to provide a thermo color code analysis. The more green, the closer the organization is on track to becoming an employer of choice.

Thermo Analysis:

Green = Evidence is in place and to desired level. Organization is committed to quality control and has a process and standards in place to ensure this area stays green.

Yellow = Foundation started; however, this area needs attention to demonstrate evidence.

Red = Area determined to be a risk and has the potential to negatively influence attraction and retention.

Note: All evidence must be observable, measurable, and definable. For example, if you check green in a box, be prepared to show your evidence if asked. The point is to avoid assumption and be fact-oriented.

Organizational Maturity	Cultural Reality	Employee Job Satisfaction Hygiene Factors (lead to dissatisfaction)	Employee Job Satisfaction Motivational Factors (lead to employee satisfaction)
□ Defined Employee Value Proposition	□ Money vs. meaningful work	□ Working conditions	□ Personal achievement
□ Effective executive leadership capacity	□ Corporate values vs. assumptions	□ Quality of supervision	□ Recognition for achievement
□ Performance management	□ Respect vs. lack of trust	□ Compensation package	□ Responsibility for tasks
□ Quality of communications	□ Organizational co-operation	□ Employment status	□ Interest in job
□ Effective supervisory style	□ Organizational commitment	□ Job security	□ Advancement to higher level tasks
□ Commitment to quality	□ Level of fear	□ Company brand	□ Personal growth recognition for achievement
□ Ability to transfer knowledge	□ Open to generational differences	□ Job function	□ Career path
□ Proven ability to manage change	□ Evaluating performance attitudes	□ Company politics	
	□ Corporate brand in marketplace	□ Interpersonal relationships	

Triangulation Theory Strategic Plan

For areas that are yellow or red based on the Triangulation Theory Thermo Gap Analysis, in this phase the organization will align a strategic plan that prioritizes its short-term (60 days), mid-term (1 year) and long-term goals (3 years) to develop a core element. For each goal, describe the end outcome, measures of success, and actions. The purpose of short- and mid-term goals is to show the steps necessary to achieve a long-term goal. Organizational change is a process.

Organizational Maturity	Thermo Analysis □ Red □ Yellow	Short-term (60 days)	Mid-term (1 year)	Long-term goals (3 years)
Cultural Reality		Short-term (60 days)	Mid-term (1 year)	Long-term goals (3 years)
Employee Job Satisfaction Hygiene Factors		Short-term (60 days)	Mid-term (1 year)	Long-term goals (3 years)
Employee Job Satisfaction Motivational Factors		Short-term (60 days)	Mid-term (1 year)	Long-term goals (3 years)

APPENDIX B

Branham's 54-Summary Checklist of Employer of Choice Engagement Process

To build a strategic plan for becoming an employer of choice it's important to be aware that it's often not responsible or possible to do everything at once. The below list provides an overview of core behaviors that an employer could consider doing to enhance a particular core area that was found as a gap in the Triangulation Theory Thermo Gap Analysis. Branham (2005) suggests corporate leaders use this list as a checklist to measure what they are doing well and what can be improved and then determine priorities and order of action. The list below provides ideas, but it's up to the employer to do the research needed to make each of idea come to life within the organization. There are no quick fixes and every organization will need to learn with its workforce what works and what does not. Becoming an employer of choice is a process, not an event.

To Match Candidate Expectation with Work Realities (Aligned well with Job Satisfaction Element)

1. Conduct realistic job previews with every job candidate.
2. Hire from pool of temps, adjunct staff, interims, and part-time workers.
3. Hire candidates referred by current employees.
4. Create a realistic job description with a short list of most critical competencies.
5. Allow team members to interview candidates.
6. Hire from a pool of current employees.
7. Create a way for candidates to sample the work experience.
8. Survey or interview new hires to find out how to minimize new-hire surprise in the future.

To Match the Person to the Job (Aligned well with Organizational Maturity Element)

9. Make a strong commitment to continue upgrading talent.
10. See that all hiring managers perform talent forecasting.
11. Cast a wide recruiting net to expand the universe of best-fit candidates.
12. Track and measure hiring success.
13. Align functions and tasks to the right people.
14. Conduct entrance interviews with all new hires.
15. Enrich the jobs of all employees.
16. Delegate tasks to challenge employees and enrich jobs.

To Provide Coaching and Feedback (Aligned well with all Three Core Elements)

17. Provide intensive feedback and coaching to new hires.
18. Create a culture of continuous feedback and coaching.
19. Train managers in performance coaching.
20. Make the performance management process less controlling and more of a partnership.
21. Terminate non-performers when best efforts to coach or reassign don't pay off.
22. Hold managers accountable for coaching and giving feedback.
23. Provide career advancement and growth opportunities.
24. Provide self-assessment tools and career self-management training for all employees.
25. Offer career coaching tools and training for all managers.
26. Provide readily acceptable information on career paths and competency requirements.
27. Keep employees informed about the company's strategy, direction, and talent need forecasts.
28. Build and maintain a fair and efficient internal job posting process.
29. Show clear preference for hiring from within.
30. Eliminate HR policies and management practices that block internal involvement.
31. Create a strong mentoring culture.
32. Keep career development and performance appraisal processes separate.

33. Build an effective talent review and succession management process.
34. Maintain a strong commitment to employee training.

To Make Employees Feel Valued and Recognized (Aligned well with Job Satisfaction Element)

35. Offer competitive base pay linked to value creation.
36. Reward results with variable pay aligned with business goals.
37. Reward employees at a high enough level to motivate higher performance.
38. Use cash payout for on-the-spot recognition.
39. Involve employees and encourage two-way communication when designing new pay systems.
40. Monitor the pay system to ensure fairness, efficiency, consistency, and accuracy.
41. Create a culture of informal recognition founded on sincere appreciation.
42. Make new hires feel welcome and important.
43. Ask for employee input, then listen and respond.
44. Keep employees in the loop.
45. Provide the right tools and resources.
46. Keep the physical environment fit to work in.

To Reduce Stress from Work-Life Imbalance and Overwork (Aligned well with Cultural Reality)

47. Initiate a culture of giving before getting.
48. Tailor the culture of giving to the needs of the key talent.
49. Build a culture that values spontaneous acts of caring.
50. Build social connectedness and cohesion among employees.
51. Encourage fun in the workplace.

To Inspire Trust and Confidence in Senior Leaders (Aligned well with Cultural Reality)

52. Inspire confidence in a clear vision, a workable plan, and the competence to achieve it.
53. Back up words with actions.
54. Pace your trust and confidence in your workforce.

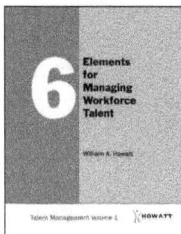

9 Elements for Integrated Performance Management is Volume 4 in the Howatt HR Consulting Talent Management Series. Each of the nine elements provides organizations with core components needed to develop an effective performance management model.

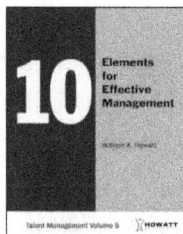

6 Elements for Managing Workforce Talent is Volume 1 of Howatt HR Consulting's Talent Management Series that has been developed to promote strategic talent management considerations. Volume 1 introduces six elements that help companies enhance their talent equity — the accumulated value an organization gains from its workforce.

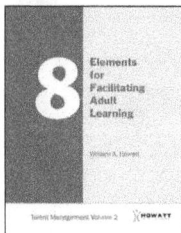

10 Elements for Effective Management is Volume 5 in the Howatt HR Consulting Talent Management Series. Each of the 10 elements provides leaders with competencies to discover strategies and tools to be more effective in implementing their vision through their people.

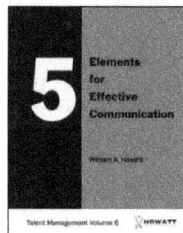

8 Elements for Facilitating Adult Learning is Volume 2 of Howatt HR Consulting's Talent Management Series that promotes strategic considerations for developing effective structured and planned professional programs. Vol. 2 explores considerations for adult learning design and delivery.

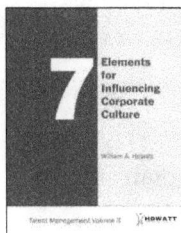

5 Elements for Effective Communication is Volume 6 in the Howatt HR Consulting Talent Management Series. Each of the five elements explores the art and the science of effective communication and the strategies for managing it that bring health to individuals and their organizations.

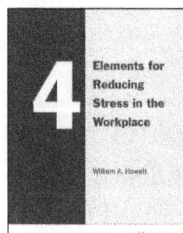

7 Elements for Influencing Corporate Culture is the Volume 3 in the Howatt HR Consulting Talent Management Series. Each of the seven elements has been developed to provide corporate leaders with insight and strategies for enhancing corporate culture.

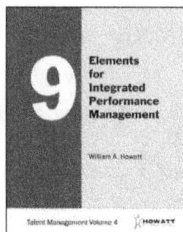

4 Elements for Reducing Stress in the Workplace is Volume 7 in the Howatt HR Consulting Talent Management Series. Each of the four elements examines the role and impact of stress in the workplace and what organizations can do to reduce and manage stress.

Why They Stay and Why They Go –

The Facts Behind Employee Retention

1-Day Workshop
Presented by
Howatt HR Consulting

The Challenge

Companies paying attention to the tangible and intangible costs associated with employee turnover understand the cost of turnover in both money and time. These companies are starting to address the challenges associated with improving employee retention.

Who is this Workshop for?

This program is for companies looking for strategies to slow down employee turnover. Clearly, turnover will never be eliminated; in fact, it is needed to ensure companies don't keep the wrong employees. However, in regard to good employees, much can be done to slow retention. We invite companies to send managers from all levels so collectively their leaders can initiate actions needed for change.

Program Objectives

- Examine why employees stay.
- Explore what motivates employees.
- Understand why most employees leave.
- Discuss the link between attraction and retention.
- Define the role of leadership at all levels.
- Demonstrate the influence of culture in turnover.
- Calculate the benefits of retention.
- Show how teamwork facilitates retention.
- Learn strategies for improving retention.
- Formulate an action plan for addressing turnover.

Contact

Howatt HR Consulting

to arrange a 1-day workshop for

Senior Managers in your organization

info@howatthr.com

902-678-8668

HOWATT
HR CONSULTING INC.

Meet The Author

William A. Howatt

PhD, EdD, Post Doc Behavioral Science UCLA School of Medicine

is recognized as an international strategic **HR** expert who works with organizations throughout the world to develop their most valuable resource—their human capital. Through his commitment to excellence, passion for learning, and teaching with a dash of humor he works with organizations and teams to achieve results in their quest to manage and develop their talent.

Dr. Bill has been helping companies to discover attraction and retention solutions to better align their people with their business. He uses a simple formula to help companies define in real dollars what it is costing to do nothing and the potential risk. His approach is clear and logical to help organizations meet complex people issues head on and find solutions that work.

Dr. Bill is a business columnist and has an extensive publishing history. He has an extensive academic and professional background that he uses in his consulting solutions.

For a full listing of Howatt HR Consulting books and guides, visit www.howatthr.com.

HOWATT
HR CONSULTING INC.

What is the cost of doing nothing?

www.ingramcontent.com/pod-product-compliance
Lightning Source LLC
Chambersburg PA
CBHW060618200326
41521CB00007B/804